EXOTIC COOKERY

Edited by Norma MacMillan and Wendy James
Home economist Gilly Cubitt

ORBIS PUBLISHING London

Introduction

Take a trip around the world without leaving home. The recipes in this book enable you to try out the exotic cuisines of China and the Far East, the Caribbean, Arabia and India in your own kitchen!

Both imperial and metric measures are given for each recipe; you should follow only one set of measures as they are not direct conversions. All spoon measures are level unless otherwise stated. Pastry quantities are based on the amount of flour used. Dried herbs may be substituted for fresh herbs; use one-third of the quantity.

Photographs were supplied by Editions Atlas, Editions Atlas/Masson, Editions Atlas/Zadora, Archivio IGDA, Lavinia Press Agency, Orbis GmbH

The material in this book has previously appeared in *The Complete Cook*

First published 1981 in Great Britain by Orbis Publishing Limited, 20–22 Bedfordbury, London WC2

ISBN 0-85613-374-4
Printed in Singapore

Contents

Chinese spring rolls

Overall timing 1½ hours plus resting

Freezing Suitable: fill and cook after thawing

Makes 12

8 oz	Strong plain flour	225 g
½ teasp	Salt	2.5 ml
4	Eggs	4
	Cornflour	
	Oil for frying	
Filling		
8 oz	Lean pork	225 g
2 tbsp	Oil	2x15 ml
4	Spring onions	4
2 oz	Mushrooms	50 g
4 oz	Shelled shrimps	125 g
8 oz	Bean sprouts	225 g
2 tbsp	Soy sauce	2x15 ml
1 teasp	Sugar	5 ml
	Salt	

Sift flour and salt into a bowl. Add three eggs and mix with fingers to a soft dough. Knead for at least 10 minutes till smooth and elastic. Rest for 2 hours.

Meanwhile, make the filling. Thinly slice pork across the grain, cut into strips and fry in oil for 2 minutes. Trim and slice spring onions and mushrooms. Add to the pan with shrimps, bean sprouts and soy sauce, and stir-fry for 2 minutes. Add sugar and salt, mix well and leave to cool.

Divide dough in half. Dredge board with cornflour and roll out half dough till very thin. Stretch it further with back of hands till transparent. Cut into six 6 inch (15cm) squares. Place a square with one corner towards you. Put a little filling across centre. Fold bottom corner up and side corners in over filling. Brush open flap with beaten egg. Roll up, finishing with point under. Repeat to make 12 rolls

Heat oil in a deep-fryer to 350°F (170°C) and fry spring rolls for 3–4 minutes till crisp and golden. Drain on kitchen paper and serve hot.

Bird's nest soup

Overall timing 50 minutes plus overnight soaking

Freezing Not suitable

To serve 4–6

4 oz	Dried swallow's nest	125 g
2 pints	Boiling water	1.1 litres
2 pints	Home-made chicken stock	1.1 litres
2 tbsp	Dry sherry	2x15 ml
	Salt and pepper	

Put bird's nest into a bowl. Pour boiling water over and leave to soak overnight.

Next day, drain nest well and pick over. Put into a saucepan, add stock and bring to the boil. Cover and simmer for 20 minutes.

Remove soup from heat and stir in sherry and seasoning. Serve immediately, either as a hot starter or as part of a complete Chinese meal.

Celeriac soup

Overall timing 1 hour 20 minutes

Freezing Suitable: add noodles and celeriac after reheating

To serve 4

½ oz	Chinese dried mushrooms	15 g
8 oz	Pork fillet	225 g
2	Onions	2
1	Garlic clove	1
1¼ lb	Celeriac	600 g
4 tbsp	Oil	4x15 ml
1½ pints	Chicken stock	850 ml
1 oz	Chinese vermicelli	25 g
2 tbsp	Soy sauce	2x15 ml
	Ground ginger	
	Salt and pepper	

Soak mushrooms in warm water for 30 minutes.

Finely slice pork. Peel and finely chop onions and garlic. Cut the tops off the celeriac and save a few small leaves for garnish. Peel celeriac and chop into ½ inch (12.5 mm) cubes.

Heat the oil in a saucepan and stir-fry pork for 3 minutes. Add onions, garlic and celeriac and cook for a further 5 minutes. Drain mushrooms, remove stalks, halve or quarter them according to size and add to pan with the stock. Cover the pan, bring to the boil and simmer for 20 minutes.

Add the noodles and cook for further 5 minutes. Add washed and chopped celeriac leaves, soy sauce and a pinch of ground ginger. Cook for a further 5 minutes, then adjust seasoning and serve.

Hot-sour soup with bean curd

Overall timing 1 hour plus soaking

Freezing Not suitable

To serve 4

1 oz	Chinese dried mushrooms	25 g
4 oz	Lean pork, beef or boned chicken	125 g
1 oz	Canned bamboo shoots	25 g
2	Bean curd cakes	2
2 pints	Stock	1.1 litres
2 tbsp	Vinegar	2x15 ml
2 tbsp	Soy sauce	2x15 ml
2 tbsp	Cornflour	2x15 ml
	Black pepper	
2	Eggs	2

Soak the mushrooms in warm water for 30 minutes. Slice meat into thin strips. Chop bamboo shoots and bean curd.

Drain mushrooms, reserving 2 tbsp (2x 15 ml) of soaking liquid. Remove stalks, then slice mushrooms into strips. Put into saucepan with reserved soaking liquid, stock, meat and bamboo shoots. Bring to the boil and simmer for 30 minutes.

Mix together vinegar, soy sauce, cornflour and pepper. Beat eggs in another bowl.

Add bean curd to soup and simmer for 5 minutes. Stir in vinegar mixture and simmer, stirring, till soup thickens. Gently trickle in eggs, then serve immediately.

Cantonese fish soup

Overall timing 35 minutes plus marination

Freezing Not suitable

To serve 6

12 oz	White fish fillets	350 g
2 tbsp	Soy sauce	2x15 ml
2 teasp	Dry sherry	2x5 ml
3 tbsp	Oil	3x15 ml
2	Medium onions	2
4	Shallots	4
2	Medium carrots	2
3	Stalks of celery	3
2½ pints	Chicken stock	1.5 litres
2 oz	Long grain rice	50 g
	Salt and pepper	

Cut across the fillets into thin strips and put into a bowl. Add the soy sauce, sherry and 1 tbsp (15 ml) of the oil. Mix well and leave to marinate in a cool place for 1 hour.

Peel and chop the onions and two of the shallots. Peel and dice the carrots. Trim and chop the celery. Heat remaining oil in a large saucepan, add prepared vegetables, cover and cook gently for 5 minutes. Add the stock and bring to the boil. Stir in rice and salt, bring back to the boil, cover and simmer for 10 minutes.

Add the fish and marinating juices and cook for a further 10 minutes. Taste and adjust seasoning. Pour into soup bowls and garnish with remaining shallots, peeled and finely chopped.

Chinese noodles with cabbage

Overall timing 1 hour including marination

Freezing Not suitable

To serve 4

1½ oz	Chinese dried mushrooms	40 g
8 oz	Shelled prawns	225 g
2 tbsp	Soy sauce	2x15 ml
1 tbsp	Dry sherry	15 ml
1 tbsp	Chopped root ginger	15 ml
1 tbsp	Cornflour	15 ml
12 oz	Green cabbage	350 g
4 oz	Can of bamboo shoots	125 g
5 tbsp	Oil	5x15 ml
	Salt	
11 oz	Chinese vermicelli	300 g

Soak mushrooms in warm water for 30 minutes. Put prawns in a bowl with soy sauce, sherry, ginger and cornflour. Leave for 20 minutes.

Drain mushrooms, remove stalks and chop. Cut cabbage into thin strips. Drain and slice bamboo shoots. Heat 2 tbsp (2x15 ml) oil in frying pan and stir-fry mushrooms, cabbage and bamboo shoots for 2 minutes. Sprinkle with salt and transfer to a bowl.

Add 1 tbsp (15 ml) oil to pan and cook prawns and marinade for 3 minutes. Return cabbage mixture and stir-fry for 5 minutes.

Cook noodles in boiling salted water for 8 minutes, then drain well. Heat remaining oil in another frying pan and stir-fry noodles for a few minutes. Add noodles to other ingredients. Cook and stir-fry for a further 4 minutes. Transfer to a warmed serving dish and serve hot.

Mushroom soup

Overall timing 30 minutes

Freezing Not suitable

To serve 4

2	Stalks of celery	2
8 oz	Mushrooms	225 g
2 teasp	Oil	2x5 ml
12 oz	Cooked chicken meat	350 g
1 tbsp	Soy sauce	15 ml
1 tbsp	Dry sherry	15 ml
8	Water chestnuts	8
1¾ pints	Chicken stock	1 litre
4 oz	Bean sprouts	125 g
	Salt and pepper	
1	Egg	1

Finely chop celery. Thinly slice mushrooms. Heat oil in a saucepan and stir-fry vegetables for 5 minutes.

Cut chicken into small pieces and sprinkle with soy sauce and sherry. Quarter or dice water chestnuts.

Add stock to pan with water chestnuts. Bring to the boil, then add chicken and soaking juices. Simmer for 10 minutes. Add bean sprouts and cook for 2 minutes. Taste and adjust seasoning.

Beat egg. Remove pan from heat and trickle in beaten egg, stirring constantly. Divide soup between individual soup bowls and serve.

Chicken vermicelli soup

Overall timing 40 minutes

Freezing Not suitable

To serve 6

1 oz	Chinese dried mushrooms	25 g
2½ pints	Chicken stock	1.5 litres
6 oz	Cooked chicken meat	175 g
2	Lettuce leaves	2
4	Eggs	4
	Salt and pepper	
1 oz	Butter	25 g
2 oz	Chinese vermicelli	50 g
2 tbsp	Dry sherry	2x15 ml

Soak mushrooms in warm water for 30 minutes. Drain, discard woody stalks and put into saucepan with stock. Bring to the boil and simmer for 10 minutes.

Meanwhile, cut chicken into strips. Shred lettuce. Beat eggs with seasoning. Melt half butter in frying pan, add half egg mixture and make a thin omelette. Remove from pan and reserve. Use remaining butter and egg mixture to make another omelette. Roll up both omelettes and cut into thin slices.

Add noodles and chicken to saucepan and simmer for 2 minutes. Remove from heat and add sherry, omelette strips and lettuce. Serve immediately.

Chicken with pineapple

Overall timing 30 minutes

Freezing Not suitable

To serve 4

4	Boned chicken breasts	4
2 tbsp	Vegetable oil	2x15 ml
¼ teasp	Ground ginger	1.25 ml
15½ oz	Can of pineapple rings	439 g
	Salt and pepper	
1 teasp	Cornflour	5 ml
1 tbsp	Soy sauce	15 ml
2 teasp	White wine vinegar	2x5 ml

Cut chicken into neat pieces. Heat oil in a frying pan and fry chicken with ginger for 5 minutes, turning frequently.

Drain pineapple rings, reserving syrup. Cut three rings into chunks and add to chicken with seasoning. Cover and cook for a further 5 minutes.

Blend cornflour with soy sauce, vinegar and ¼ pint (150 ml) pineapple syrup. Pour over chicken and bring to the boil, stirring. Cook gently for 5 minutes.

Meanwhile, cut remaining pineapple rings in half and warm gently in remaining syrup. Arrange chicken on a warmed serving dish and garnish with halved pineapple rings.

Cantonese rice

Overall timing 50 minutes

Freezing Not suitable

To serve 4

6	Dried Chinese mushrooms	6
2	Small onions	2
8 oz	Streaky bacon	225 g
8 oz	Roast pork or chicken meat	225 g
3 tbsp	Oil	3x15 ml
1 lb	Cooked rice	450 g
4 oz	Shelled prawns	125 g
1 tbsp	Chopped chives	15 ml
	Salt and pepper	
¼ teasp	Cayenne pepper	1.25 ml
2	Eggs	2

Soak mushrooms in warm water for 30 minutes. Peel onions and cut into thin wedges. Derind and dice bacon; finely shred pork or chicken. Drain and chop mushrooms, discarding stalks.

Heat oil in frying pan and stir-fry onions, mushrooms, bacon and meat for 3–4 minutes. Add rice and stir-fry for 1 minute. Stir in prawns, chives, salt and cayenne; cook for 3 minutes.

Meanwhile, beat eggs with seasoning and 1 tbsp (15 ml) cold water. Make a thin omelette, roll up and shred finely. Pile rice mixture on warmed serving dish and top with omelette.

Fried prawns in shells

Overall timing 20 minutes

Freezing Not suitable

To serve 4

1 lb	Raw prawns	450 g
2	Spring onions	2
2	Garlic cloves	2
4 tbsp	Oil	4 x 15 ml
2 tbsp	Soy sauce	2 x 15 ml
2 tbsp	Sherry	2 x 15 ml
1 teasp	Sugar	5 ml
1 teasp	Vinegar	5 ml
$\frac{1}{2}$ teasp	Salt	2.5 ml

Carefully remove the heads and legs from prawns, leaving on shells and tails. Wash and drain. Trim the onions and cut into 2 inch (5 cm) lengths. Peel and crush the garlic.

Heat the oil in a frying pan. When very hot add prawns and stir-fry over a moderate heat for 2 minutes. Add the onions, garlic, soy sauce, sherry, sugar, vinegar and salt and stir-fry for a further 2 minutes till shells are crispy. Pour mixture into a warmed serving dish and serve immediately with rice and salad.

Meatballs and spinach

Overall timing 45 minutes

Freezing Not suitable

To serve 4

1 lb	Minced pork	450 g
1 tbsp	Chopped chives	15 ml
1	Egg	1
2 tbsp	Soy sauce	2×15 ml
4 tbsp	Oil	4×15 ml
2 tbsp	Dry sherry	2×15 ml
$\frac{1}{4}$ pint	Water	150 ml
2 lb	Spinach	900 g
1 teasp	Cornflour	5 ml
	Salt and pepper	

Pound minced pork with chives, egg and half the soy sauce till mixture binds together. Shape into eight balls.

Heat half the oil in a frying pan, add the meatballs and fry over a medium heat for 10 minutes, turning till browned. Add the remaining soy sauce, the sherry and water, bring to the boil, cover and simmer for 15 minutes.

Meanwhile, shred the spinach. Heat the remaining oil in another frying pan, add the spinach and stir-fry over a high heat for 3 minutes.

Blend the cornflour with 1 tbsp (15 ml) cold water and add to the meatballs. Bring to the boil, stirring till thickened. Season to taste.

Arrange the spinach on a warmed serving dish and place the meatballs on top. Spoon the sauce over the meatballs and serve with a side dish of soy sauce.

Pork with bamboo shoots

Overall timing 50 minutes

Freezing Not suitable

To serve 4

12 oz	Pork fillet	350 g
1 teasp	Salt	5 ml
2 teasp	Sugar	2x5 ml
2 tbsp	Soy sauce	2x15 ml
3 tbsp	Sake or dry sherry	3x15 ml
4 oz	Button mushrooms	125 g
2	Stalks of celery	2
1	Onion	1
10 oz	Can of bamboo shoots	283 g
$\frac{1}{4}$ teasp	Monosodium glutamate	1.25 ml
3 tbsp	Oil	3x15 ml
	Sprigs of parsley	

Cut pork into very thin slices across the grain. Put the pork into a bowl with the salt, sugar, soy sauce and sake or sherry. Mix well and leave to marinate for 30 minutes.

Meanwhile, slice the mushrooms. Trim the celery and slice diagonally. Peel and slice the onion. Drain the bamboo shoots and cut into strips. Place vegetables in a bowl. Sprinkle with monosodium glutamate and leave for 15 minutes.

Drain the pork, reserving the marinade. Heat the oil in frying pan and stir-fry the pork for 4–5 minutes. Add the prepared vegetables and stir-fry for 3 minutes. Add the reserved marinade and cook for a further 3 minutes.

Pile the mixture into a warmed serving dish, garnish with parsley sprigs and serve immediately with boiled egg noodles or with plain boiled rice.

Cantonese roast pork

Overall timing 2½ hours plus marination

Freezing Not suitable

To serve 6

2½ lb	Boned fillet end of leg of pork	1.1 kg
2 tbsp	Soy sauce	2x15 ml
2 tbsp	Hoisin sauce	2x15 ml
2 tbsp	Honey	2x15 ml
1 tbsp	Caster sugar	15 ml
2 tbsp	Dry sherry	2x15 ml
	Salt	
3 tbsp	Sesame oil	3x15 ml
¼ pint	Chicken stock	150 ml
1	Star anise	1

Remove skin from pork, leaving a thin layer of fat on the meat. Tie into a neat shape with fine string. Put into a bowl. Mix together the soy and hoisin sauces, honey, sugar, sherry and salt, and rub all over the pork. Cover and marinate in a cool place for 1 hour, turning occasionally.

Preheat the oven to 400°F (200°C) Gas 6.

Heat the sesame oil in a flameproof casserole and fry the pork over a high heat till lightly browned on all sides. Add any marinade left in the bowl, the stock and star anise, and bring to the boil. Baste the pork, then cover and cook in the oven for about 1¾ hours, basting the pork every 15 minutes.

Place the pork on a warmed serving plate and discard the string. Carve into thick slices and serve with boiled rice garnished with Chinese mushrooms, and bamboo shoots and beansprouts stir-fried together.

Sweet and sour pork

Overall timing 40 minutes plus marination

Freezing Suitable

To serve 4

1 lb	Lean pork	450 g
2 tbsp	Dry sherry	2x15 ml
	Salt and pepper	
1	Egg	1
3 tbsp	Plain flour	3x15 ml
3 tbsp	Oil	3x15 ml
2	Carrots	2
2	Onions	2
1	Large cucumber	1
1	Garlic clove	1
4 tbsp	Tomato ketchup	4x15 ml
2 teasp	Soy sauce	2x5 ml
2 tbsp	Vinegar	2x15 ml
1 tbsp	Brown sugar	15 ml
1 tbsp	Cornflour	15 ml
½ pint	Water	300 ml

Cut meat into ½ inch (12.5 mm) cubes. Put into a bowl with sherry and seasoning and marinate for 30 minutes.

Lightly beat egg. Dip pork cubes in egg, then coat with flour. Heat oil in a large frying pan. Fry pork for 8 minutes till golden brown on all sides. Remove from pan.

Peel and chop carrots, onions and cucumber. Peel and crush garlic. Add all to frying pan and stir-fry for 5 minutes over fairly high heat. Reduce heat to moderate. Add ketchup, soy sauce, vinegar, sugar, cornflour dissolved in water and reserved marinade to the pan. Bring to the boil and cook for 3 minutes, stirring.

Return pork to pan and cook for 3 minutes more till heated through. Serve with plain boiled rice and side dishes of tomato wedges, chunks of cucumber and a little desiccated coconut for sprinkling over the finished dish.

Chinese spare ribs

Overall timing 45 minutes

Freezing Not suitable

To serve 4

1½ lb	Pork spare ribs	700 g
2 tbsp	Oil	2x15 ml
1 tbsp	Hoisin sauce	15 ml
1 tbsp	Soy sauce	15 ml
Sauce		
½ inch	Piece of root ginger	12.5 mm
1	Green pepper	1
2	Garlic cloves	2
2 tbsp	Oil	2x15 ml
1 tbsp	Soy sauce	15 ml
2 tbsp	Dry sherry	2x15 ml
2 tbsp	Tomato purée	2x15 ml
2 tbsp	Vinegar	2x15 ml
2 tbsp	Sugar	2x15 ml
1 tbsp	Cornflour	15 ml
4 tbsp	Pineapple juice	4x15 ml
3 tbsp	Water	3x15 ml

Separate the pork into ribs. Cook in boiling water for 15 minutes, then drain and dry on kitchen paper.

Heat oil in frying pan. Add ribs and stir in hoisin and soy sauces. Cook gently for 20 minutes.

Meanwhile, prepare sauce. Shred ginger. Deseed pepper and cut into thin strips. Peel and crush garlic. Heat oil in a saucepan, add garlic, ginger and pepper and stir-fry for 2 minutes. Remove from heat and stir in soy sauce, sherry, tomato purée, vinegar and sugar. Blend cornflour with fruit juice and water and add to the pan. Bring to the boil and cook for 2 minutes, stirring constantly.

Place ribs in a warmed serving dish. Pour sauce over and serve immediately with boiled rice.

Cauliflower with noodles

Overall timing 50 minutes

Freezing Not suitable

To serve 4

1	Small cauliflower	1
8 oz	Lean pork	225 g
1	Onion	1
2 tbsp	Oil	2x15 ml
2 tbsp	Soy sauce	2x15 ml
	Salt	
9 fl oz	Stock	250 ml
8 oz	Egg noodles	225 g
1 teasp	Cornflour	5 ml
	Chopped parsley	

Remove leaves and trim cauliflower stalk. Separate cauliflower into florets. Cut pork into small thin pieces. Peel and chop onion.

Heat 1 tbsp (15 ml) of the oil in a large frying pan. Add cauliflower, pork, onion and soy sauce and season with salt. Cook for a few minutes. Stir in stock, cover and cook for 35 minutes.

Meanwhile, cook noodles in boiling salted water for 8 minutes. Drain well.

Mix cornflour with a little water and add to cauliflower mixture. Simmer till thickened.

Heat remaining oil in another frying pan. Stir-fry noodles for a few minutes till golden, then add to cauliflower mixture. Heat through, garnish with parsley and serve.

Pork stir-fried with vegetables

Overall timing 50 minutes

Freezing Not suitable

To serve 4

1 lb	Pork fillet	450 g
1	Leek	1
1	Garlic clove	1
4 oz	Button mushrooms	125 g
8 oz	Can of bamboo shoots	227 g
3 tbsp	Oil	3x15 ml
$\frac{1}{4}$ pint	Chicken stock	150 ml
4 oz	Frozen peas	125 g
2 teasp	Cornflour	2x5 ml
Marinade		
3 tbsp	Soy sauce	3x15 ml
3 tbsp	Dry sherry	3x15 ml
	Salt and pepper	
2 teasp	Caster sugar	2x5 ml

Slice the pork thinly across the grain, then cut into 1 inch (2.5 cm) strips. Mix ingredients for the marinade in a bowl. Add the pork, stir and marinate for 30 minutes.

Meanwhile, cut the leek into 3 inch (7.5 cm) lengths and shred. Peel and crush the garlic. Halve the mushrooms. Drain and slice bamboo shoots. Heat the oil in frying pan, add garlic, leeks and mushrooms and stir-fry over a high heat for 4 minutes.

Lift the pork out of the marinade and drain thoroughly. Add to the pan and stir-fry for 3 minutes. Stir in the stock, bring to the boil, add the peas, cover and cook for 3 minutes.

Blend the cornflour to a smooth paste with the marinade, add to the pan and bring back to the boil, stirring constantly. Simmer till thickened. Serve with boiled rice.

Pork chop suey

Overall timing 1½ hours including soaking time

Freezing Not suitable

To serve 4–6

1 lb	Pork fillet	450 g
6 tbsp	Dry sherry	6x15 ml
5 tbsp	Soy sauce	5x15 ml
	Ground ginger	
	Salt and pepper	
1 tbsp	Chinese dried mushrooms	15 ml
4 oz	Noodles	125 g
3	Stalks of celery	3
½ bunch	Spring onions	½ bunch
7½ oz	Can of bamboo shoots	213 g
8 tbsp	Vegetable oil	8x15 ml
8 oz	Bean sprouts	225 g
1 teasp	Sugar	5 ml
1 tbsp	Cornflour	15 ml

Cut pork into strips and put into bowl with 2 tbsp (2x15 ml) sherry and soy sauce, a pinch of ginger and seasoning. Leave for 1 hour. Soak mushrooms in warm water for 30 minutes.

Meanwhile, cook noodles in boiling salted water for 5 minutes. Lift out, then cook sliced celery for 5 minutes. Drain. Drain mushrooms and slice. Chop onions. Drain and slice bamboo shoots.

Heat oil in frying pan. Add pork and brown all over. Remove from pan. Add mushrooms, onions, bamboo shoots and bean sprouts and cook for 3 minutes. Stir in pork, celery, noodles, remaining soy sauce and sugar. Stir-fry for 3 minutes.

Mix together cornflour and remaining sherry and stir into chop suey. Cook for 4 minutes.

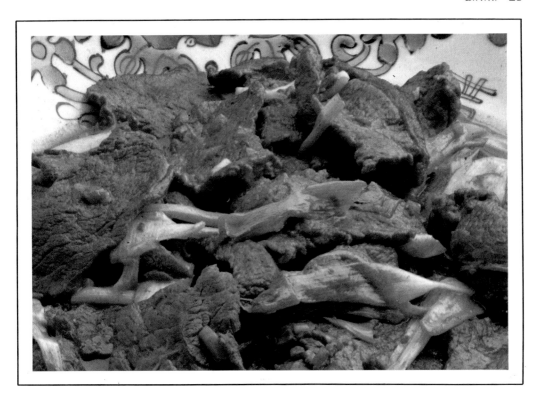

Lamb and spring onions

Overall timing 15 minutes plus marination

Freezing Not suitable

To serve 6

2 lb	Leg of lamb	900 g
2	Garlic cloves	2
2	Slices of root ginger	2
2 tbsp	Soy sauce	2x15 ml
1 tbsp	Sherry	15 ml
½ teasp	Salt	2.5 ml
4	Spring onions	4
4 tbsp	Oil	4x15 ml

Slice lamb into thin, bite-size pieces. Peel and crush the garlic; cut ginger into tiny strips. Place lamb, ginger and garlic in a bowl and add soy sauce, sherry and salt. Mix well and marinate for 30 minutes.

Slice the spring onions in half lengthways, then across into 1 inch (2.5 cm) pieces.

Heat oil in frying pan. Add lamb and marinade, increase heat and stir-fry for 2 minutes. Add spring onions and stir-fry for another minute. Serve immediately.

Sweet sour lamb riblets

Overall timing 1¼ hours plus overnight marination

Freezing Not suitable

To serve 4

1	Onion	1
2	Garlic cloves	2
2 tbsp	Honey	2x15 ml
1 tbsp	Oil	15 ml
4 tbsp	Soy sauce	4x15 ml
¼ pint	Dry sherry	150 ml
1 teasp	Ground ginger	5 ml
2 oz	Caster sugar	50 g
1 teasp	Ground allspice	5 ml
2½ lb	Breast of lamb riblets	1.1 kg

Peel and slice onion. Peel and crush garlic. Put into a bowl with the honey, oil, soy sauce, sherry, ginger, sugar and allspice. Add the breast riblets, cover and marinate overnight in the refrigerator, turning occasionally.

The next day, preheat the oven to 375°F (190°C) Gas 5.

Put the meat into a roasting tin and spoon the marinade over. Bake for 1 hour, basting frequently with the marinade. Serve with plain boiled rice.

Stir-fried liver and cabbage

Overall timing 40 minutes

Freezing Not suitable

To serve 4

1 lb	Lamb's liver	450 g
	Salt and pepper	
2 oz	Plain flour	50 g
5 tbsp	Sunflower oil	5 x 15 ml
1	Large onion	1
1	Red pepper	1
1	Green pepper	1
3 teasp	Soy sauce	3 x 5 ml
2 tbsp	Medium sherry	2 x 15 ml
4 fl oz	Stock	120 ml
7 oz	Savoy cabbage	200 g
8 oz	Bean sprouts	225 g
4 oz	Can of bamboo shoots	125 g

Cut liver into thin strips and coat in seasoned flour. Heat oil in frying pan, add liver strips and fry for about 10 minutes. Remove from pan and keep warm.

Peel and slice onion, add to pan and fry for 5 minutes. Deseed and slice peppers. Add to pan with soy sauce, sherry and stock. Cook for 5 minutes.

Cut cabbage into fine strips. Add to pan with bean sprouts and drained and sliced bamboo shoots. Bring to the boil and cook, stirring, for 5 minutes. Return the liver to the pan and cook for a further 1–2 minutes until heated through. Serve immediately.

Chicken chow mein

Overall timing 45 minutes including soaking

Freezing Not suitable

To serve 4

½ oz	Chinese dried mushrooms	15 g
1 lb	Chinese vermicelli	450 g
	Salt	
4 tbsp	Oil	4x15 ml
4 oz	Chicken breast	125 g
8 oz	Broccoli spears	225 g
3	Spring onions	3
3 tbsp	Soy sauce	3x15 ml
2 tbsp	Dry sherry	2x15 ml
1 teasp	Sugar	5 ml
1 teasp	Sesame oil	5 ml

Soak mushrooms in warm water for 30 minutes. Cook noodles in boiling salted water for 3–5 minutes till tender. Drain. Mix in 1 teasp (5 ml) oil to prevent noodles sticking together.

Slice the chicken into long thin strips, discarding skin. Cut broccoli into 2 inch (5 cm) lengths. Trim onions and chop into 1 inch (2.5 cm) pieces. Mix together soy sauce, ½ teasp (2.5 ml) salt, the sherry and sugar. Drain mushrooms, discard stalks and cut into thin strips.

Heat 2 tbsp (2x15 ml) oil in frying pan. Add chicken, mushrooms, onions and broccoli and stir-fry for 2 minutes. Add half sherry mixture and stir-fry for 1 minute. Tip mixture into a warmed dish and keep hot.

Heat remaining oil in pan, add noodles and fry for 2 minutes. Add some of the meat mixture and fry for 1 minute. Tip on to a warmed serving dish.

Place remaining meat mixture in pan with rest of sherry mixture and stir-fry for 30 seconds. Mix in sesame oil and arrange on top of noodles.

Mandarin chicken

Overall timing 1 hour

Freezing Not suitable

To serve 4

2 oz	Sultanas	50 g
¼ pint	Madeira	150 ml
	Salt and pepper	
2 teasp	Paprika	2x5 ml
3 lb	Chicken joints	1.4 kg
5 tbsp	Oil	5x15 ml
10 oz	Can of mandarin oranges	312 g
1	Garlic clove	1
4 fl oz	Chicken stock	120 ml
1 tbsp	Cornflour	15 ml
2 tbsp	Soy sauce	2x15 ml
½ teasp	Ground ginger	2.5 ml
4 fl oz	Carton of double cream	113 ml
1 oz	Butter	25 g
2 oz	Flaked almonds	50 g

Soak sultanas in Madeira..Mix together salt, pepper and paprika and pat on to chicken joints. Heat oil in frying pan and brown chicken all over.

Drain oranges, reserving 4 fl oz (120 ml) syrup and pour it into pan. Peel and chop garlic and add to pan with stock. Bring to the boil, cover and simmer for 30 minutes.

Add sultanas and Madeira and simmer for a further 10 minutes. Transfer chicken to warmed serving dish. Mix cornflour with a little warm water, stir into pan juices and simmer till thickened. Add soy sauce, ginger, oranges and cream and heat gently.

Melt butter in a small pan and fry almonds till brown. Pour sauce over chicken and sprinkle with almonds.

Chicken with almonds

Overall timing 1 hour

Freezing Not suitable

To serve 4–5

2½–3 lb	Ovenready chicken	about 1.3 kg
1 tbsp	Potato flour or cornflour	15 ml
3 tbsp	Soy sauce	3x15 ml
1 teasp	Caster sugar	5 ml
	Salt and pepper	
2 tbsp	Oil	2x15 ml
4 oz	Split almonds	125 g
2 tbsp	Water or chicken stock	2x15 ml

Remove skin from chicken. With a sharp knife, cut all flesh from carcass then slice it into small strips. In a bowl mix together potato flour or cornflour, soy sauce, caster sugar and seasoning. Add chicken pieces and coat well.

Heat 1 tbsp (15 ml) oil in a heavy-based saucepan and gently brown almonds, turning them occasionally. Drain and reserve.

Pour remaining oil into the saucepan. Add chicken pieces and cook over a fairly high heat for 15 minutes, continually turning the chicken over. When chicken is golden brown, return almonds to pan and add water or chicken stock. Adjust seasoning, cover and cook for a further 5 minutes. Serve with boiled rice.

Crispy chicken and celery salad

Overall timing 1½ hours plus cooling

Freezing Not suitable

To serve 6

3 lb	Ovenready chicken	1.4 kg
1	Medium onion	1
	Salt and pepper	
1	Bunch of celery	1
1 tbsp	Soy sauce	15 ml
1 tbsp	Oil	15 ml
1 teasp	Sugar	5 ml

Put the chicken into large saucepan. Cover with cold water. Peel onion and add to pan with seasoning. Bring to the boil and skim off any scum. Cover and simmer for about 1 hour till tender.

Meanwhile, trim the celery and cut stalks into 2 inch (5 cm) lengths. Celery trimmings can be added to stock if liked.

Remove chicken from the stock. Bring stock back to the boil, add celery and blanch for 2 minutes. Drain celery and put into a serving dish.

Cut chicken into neat pieces, discarding skin and bones. Add to serving dish with celery and toss lightly. Mix soy sauce, oil and sugar till sugar dissolves. Spoon over the warm chicken and leave to cool completely. Toss lightly before serving.

Chicken with cashews

Overall timing 35 minutes

Freezing Not suitable

To serve 4

4 oz	Button mushrooms	125 g
1	Onion	1
3	Stalks of celery	3
4	Boned chicken breasts	4
2 tbsp	Oil	2x15 ml
	Black pepper	
2 oz	Frozen peas	50 g
2 teasp	Soy sauce	2x5 ml
¾ pint	Chicken stock	400 ml
¼ teasp	Monosodium glutamate	1.25 ml
1 tbsp	Cornflour	15 ml
1 tbsp	Dry sherry	15 ml
3 oz	Salted cashew nuts	75 g

Slice mushrooms. Peel and chop onion. Slice celery.

Cut chicken into smallish chunks. Heat oil in saucepan, add chicken and cook over a high heat, stirring, till lightly browned. Add pepper, mushrooms, onion, celery and peas and stir-fry for a few minutes. Add soy sauce and stock. Cover and simmer gently for 10–12 minutes.

Blend together the monosodium glutamate, cornflour, sherry and 1 tbsp (15 ml) of water. Stir into the chicken mixture and cook, shaking pan but not stirring, for 1–2 minutes, till juices are golden. Stir in the cashew nuts and heat for 1 minute, then serve. The dish is good served with plain boiled rice and stir-fried bean sprouts, both of which are quick to cook as well.

Chinese chicken parcels

Overall timing 1½ hours

Freezing Not suitable

To serve 4

9 oz	Boned chicken breasts	250 g
2 tbsp	Soy sauce	2x15 ml
1 tbsp	Dry sherry	15 ml
3–4	Spring onions	3–4
	Vegetable oil	
30	Thin slices root ginger	30
8 oz	Cooked green beans	225 g

Cut chicken breasts into very thin, ½ inch wide (12.5 mm) and 1 inch (2.5 cm) long strips. Place in a bowl with soy sauce and sherry. Trim spring onions and shred finely.

Cut bakewell paper into thirty 4 inch (10 cm) squares and brush with vegetable oil. Place a square with one corner pointing to you. Fold point to centre of square. Under this flap, place a few pieces of drained chicken, one piece of spring onion, one slice root ginger and one or two green beans. Fold right hand corner to centre, then left hand corner so points meet. Fold "envelope" in half to make a rectangle, then fold remaining flap to centre.

Heat vegetable oil, about 1½ inches (4 cm) deep, in deep-fryer. Carefully lower six parcels at a time into hot oil and fry for 1½ minutes on each side, turning carefully. Drain parcels on kitchen paper and serve hot.

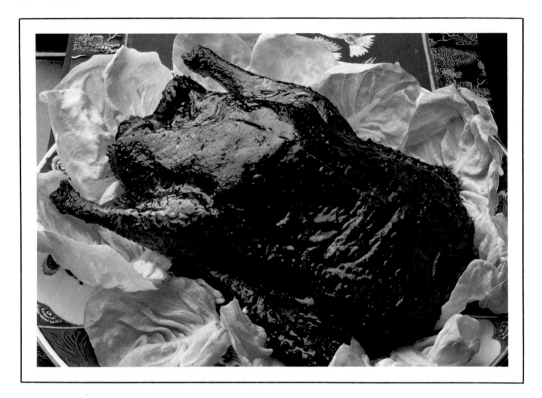

Brown-glazed duck

Overall timing 2 hours 10 minutes plus overnight cooling

Freezing Not suitable

To serve 4–6

4 lb	Ovenready duck	1.8 kg
5 tbsp	Soy sauce	5x15 ml
4 fl oz	Dry sherry	120 ml
2 tbsp	Sugar	2x15 ml
1 teasp	Five spice powder	5 ml

Preheat the oven to 350°F (180°C) Gas 4.

Prick duck all over with a fork. Place on wire rack in roasting tin and roast for 1½ hours.

Pour out juices from interior of duck and discard. Remove wire rack and drain fat from roasting tin. Mix remaining ingredients in tin. Replace duck and bring sauce to the boil on top of the stove. Baste the duck all over, then return to the oven. Roast for a further 30 minutes, basting at 5 minute intervals, until the duck takes on an even, thick and shiny glaze.

Remove duck from roasting tin, place on serving plate and cool overnight. Serve the duck cold, cut into fine strips, Chinese style, or carved, Western style.

Stir-fried celery

Overall timing 15 minutes

Freezing Not suitable

To serve 4

1	Large bunch of celery	1
2 teasp	Salt	2x5 ml
3 tbsp	Oil	3x15 ml
2 tbsp	Soy sauce	2x15 ml
$\frac{1}{2}$ teasp	Sugar	2.5 ml

Cut off leaves from celery, then chop into 2 inch (5 cm) pieces. Sprinkle with salt.

Heat oil in frying pan. When oil is very hot, add the celery and stir-fry for 5 minutes. Add soy sauce and sugar, mix well and serve immediately.

Japan and the Far East

Filipino yam soup

Overall timing 40 minutes

Freezing Not suitable

To serve 6

1½ lb	Yam or sweet potato	700 g
4 oz	Mooli or white radish	125 g
1	Large onion	1
1	Lemon	1
	Salt and pepper	
8 oz	Green beans	225 g
2	Large tomatoes	2
1	Bunch of watercress	1
2 tbsp	Anchovy essence	2x15 ml
8 oz	Shelled prawns	225 g

Peel the yam and cut into ½ inch (12.5 mm) cubes. Thinly slice the mooli. Peel and thinly slice the onion. Put 3 pints (1.7 litres) water into a saucepan and bring to the boil. Add the yam, mooli, onion, the juice of the lemon and seasoning. Bring back to the boil, then simmer for 20 minutes.

Meanwhile, top and tail the beans and cut into 2 inch (5 cm) lengths. Blanch, peel and chop the tomatoes. Trim the watercress and divide into sprigs.

Add the beans, tomatoes and anchovy essence to the pan and simmer for 5 minutes. Add the prawns and watercress and stir over a low heat for 2 minutes, then taste and adjust seasoning. Pour into a warmed tureen and serve.

Thai nam prik

Overall timing 25 minutes

Freezing Not suitable

To serve 6–8

1 inch	Cube of blachan (dried shrimp spice)	2.5 cm
2	Garlic cloves	2
3 tbsp	Lemon or lime juice	3x15 ml
1 tbsp	Caster sugar	15 ml
2 tbsp	Soy sauce	2x15 ml
	Chilli powder	
3	Stalks of celery	3
$\frac{1}{2}$	Cucumber	$\frac{1}{2}$
4 oz	Green beans	125 g
3	Carrots	3
1	Bunch of radishes	1
1	Bunch of watercress	1

Wrap the blachan in a piece of foil, place in a frying pan and fry gently, turning frequently, for 5 minutes. Remove the foil and put the blachan into a blender with the peeled garlic, fruit juice, sugar, soy sauce and a pinch of chilli powder. Blend to a smooth sauce. Pour into a small serving bowl and leave for 15 minutes.

Meanwhile, prepare the vegetables. Trim the celery, cucumber and beans and cut into 2–3 inch (5–7.5 cm) lengths, then into matchsticks. Peel the carrots and cut into sticks. Trim the radishes. Wash and drain the watercress.

Place the bowl of sauce on a serving platter, arrange the vegetables attractively around it and serve.

Gado-gado

Overall timing 30 minutes plus cooling

Freezing Not suitable

To serve 4

6 oz	Green beans	175 g
4 oz	Cabbage	125 g
2	Small cucumbers	2
2	Large tomatoes	2
$\frac{1}{2}$	Lettuce	$\frac{1}{2}$
1	Hard-boiled egg	1
Dressing		
1	Onion	1
1	Garlic clove	1
1 oz	Butter	25 g
1 teasp	Grated lemon rind	5 ml
$\frac{1}{2}$ teasp	Sugar	2.5 ml
	Pinch of salt	
1 teasp	Made mustard	5 ml
1 tbsp	Peanut butter	15 ml
3 tbsp	Double cream	3 x 15 ml
4 fl oz	Water	120 ml

Top and tail beans and cut into short lengths. Shred cabbage. Cook beans in boiling salted water for 8–10 minutes till just tender. Remove from pan with draining spoon. Add shredded cabbage to pan and blanch for 5 minutes. Drain and leave to cool.

Peel and slice cucumbers. Chop tomatoes. Shred lettuce. Shell and finely chop hard-boiled egg. Put all into a salad bowl with the cooled beans and cabbage and mix together. Chill for 15 minutes.

To make the dressing, peel and finely chop the onion and garlic. Melt the butter in a saucepan and fry the onion and garlic till transparent. Stir in the lemon rind, sugar, salt, mustard, peanut butter, cream and the water. Heat through gently for 5 minutes. Leave to cool, then pour over the salad and toss well.

Japanese mussel salad

Overall timing 30 minutes

Freezing Not suitable

To serve 4

1½ lb	Potatoes	700 g
	Salt and pepper	
2 pints	Mussels	1.1 litres
4 tbsp	Olive oil	4x15 ml
1	Garlic clove	1
¼ pint	Dry white wine	150 ml
1 tbsp	Vinegar	15 ml
	Chrysanthemum flowers (optional)	
2 tbsp	Chopped parsley	2x15 ml

Peel potatoes and cut into neat dice. Cook in boiling salted water till just tender. Drain well and put into a salad bowl.

Scrub mussels and put into a saucepan with 1 tbsp (15 ml) of the olive oil and the peeled garlic clove. Cover and cook over a high heat, shaking the pan frequently, till the mussels open. Discard any that remain closed. Remove the mussels from their shells and add to the potatoes.

Strain the cooking liquor through a muslin-lined sieve into a clean saucepan. Add the wine and vinegar to the pan and boil rapidly till reduced by half. Remove from the heat and add the remaining oil. Season to taste and pour over the salad. Mix well and sprinkle chrysanthemum flowers, if using, and chopped parsley over. Serve warm.

Spinach and egg soup

Overall timing 20 minutes

Freezing Not suitable

To serve 4

1 lb	Spinach	450 g
2	Shallots	2
2 pints	Home-made chicken stock	1.1 litres
2	Eggs	2
2 tbsp	Soy sauce	2x15 ml
	Salt and pepper	

Shred the spinach coarsely. Peel and thinly slice the shallots. Put the stock into a saucepan and bring to the boil. Skim off any scum that forms. Add the spinach and shallots and simmer for 5 minutes till the shallots are tender.

Beat the eggs lightly with a fork and add the soy sauce. Pour into the simmering soup in a thin stream, stirring constantly, so that the egg sets in strands.

Remove from the heat, season to taste, pour into individual warmed serving bowls and serve immediately.

Pork with prawns

Overall timing 50 minutes

Freezing Not suitable

To serve 4–6

1	Small onion	1
1	Garlic clove	1
3 tbsp	Oil	3x15 ml
1½ lb	Lean pork	700 g
4 oz	Shelled prawns	125 g
½ teasp	Ground ginger	2.5 ml
¼ teasp	Aniseed seeds	1.25 ml
¼ teasp	Ground cinnamon	1.25 ml
2 pints	Chicken stock	1.1 litres
1 tbsp	Vinegar	15 ml
	Salt and pepper	
10 oz	Long grain rice	275 g
1	Green pepper	1
2	Eggs	2

Peel and finely chop onion and garlic. Heat oil in saucepan and fry onion and garlic till golden.

Slice pork into strips. Add to pan and fry till browned. Add prawns and spices and fry, stirring, for 3 minutes. Add stock, vinegar and pepper and bring to the boil. Stir in rice, cover and simmer for 15–20 minutes till rice is tender.

Deseed and slice pepper. Blanch in boiling salted water for 2 minutes. Drain. Beat eggs with salt and use to make one or two thin omelettes. Roll up, cut crossways into strips and use to garnish rice with green pepper.

Japanese radish salad

Overall timing 25 minutes plus maceration

Freezing Not suitable

To serve 6

10 oz	Japanese radish	275 g
1	Cucumber	1
2 teasp	Salt	2x5 ml
1	Red-skinned apple	1
2 tbsp	Lemon juice	2x15 ml
¼ pint	Carton of soured cream	150 ml
	Black pepper	
1 teasp	Chopped fresh dill	5 ml

Peel the radish and cut into very thin slices. Thinly slice the cucumber and put into a bowl with the radish. Sprinkle with salt and macerate in the refrigerator for 30 minutes.

Core and thinly slice the apple. Put into a serving dish and sprinkle with the lemon juice to prevent discoloration.

Rinse radish and cucumber and pat dry with kitchen paper. Add to the apple and toss lightly. Lightly beat the soured cream and pepper in a bowl and pour over the salad. Sprinkle with the chopped dill and toss just before serving.

Spinach with coconut

Overall timing 1½ hours

Freezing Not suitable

To serve 4

8 fl oz	Milk	220 ml
10 oz	Fresh coconut	275 g
1	Small onion	1
1¾ lb	Fresh spinach	750 g
1 teasp	Lemon juice	5 ml
	Salt and pepper	

Put milk in a saucepan. Grate in the coconut and slowly bring to the boil. Remove pan from heat and leave to soak for 30 minutes. Strain liquid and discard coconut.

Peel and finely chop onion. Chop spinach and place in a saucepan with only the water left on the leaves after washing, the lemon juice, onion and coconut milk. Season well with salt and pepper. Cover pan and cook spinach over a low heat for 15 minutes. Serve very hot.

Rempah

Overall timing 25 minutes

Freezing Suitable: fry from frozen

To serve 4

12 oz	Finely minced beef	350 g
3 oz	Desiccated coconut	75 g
1 teasp	Ground coriander	5 ml
¼ teasp	Ground cumin	1.25 ml
1	Egg	1
	Salt and pepper	
	Oil for frying	

Place mince in a large bowl and beat in the coconut, coriander and cumin. Add the egg and seasoning and mix well to a stiff paste. Roll small pieces of the mixture between floured hands to make tightly-packed meatballs ½ inch (12.5 mm) in diameter.

Heat ½ inch (12.5 mm) oil in a frying pan and fry the meatballs for 3–5 minutes, turning frequently, till brown all over. Drain on kitchen paper and serve.

Burmese chicken with rice noodles

Overall timing 1 hour plus marination

Freezing Not suitable

To serve 4

6	Saffron strands	6
2 lb	Chicken joints	900 g
2	Large onions	2
1 inch	Piece of root ginger	2.5 cm
1	Garlic clove	1
	Chilli powder	
	Salt	
2 tbsp	Oil	2x15 ml
4 teasp	Plain flour	4x5 ml
1 pint	Coconut milk (see page 88)	560 ml
8 oz	Broad rice noodles	225 g

Put saffron into a large saucepan with chicken joints. Cover with water and bring to the boil. Skim, then cover and simmer for about 35 minutes till tender.

Remove chicken with a draining spoon and reserve. Reduce stock to 1 pint (560 ml) by rapid boiling. Cut chicken into bite-size pieces, discarding bones and skin. Peel and finely chop onions and ginger. Peel and crush garlic. Mix chicken, onions, ginger, garlic, pinch of chilli powder and salt. Leave to marinate for about 1 hour, turning from time to time.

Heat oil in another saucepan. Add chicken mixture and fry for 5 minutes, turning frequently. Add stock, and flour mixed with coconut milk. Bring to the boil, stirring and simmer for 5 minutes.

Meanwhile, cook noodles in boiling salted water for 5 minutes till tender. Drain and put into a serving dish. Pour chicken and sauce over and toss lightly to mix. Serve immediately with side dishes of chopped hard-boiled eggs, diced gherkins and sliced spring onions.

Tempura

Overall timing 25 minutes

Freezing Not suitable

To serve 6–8

1¼ lb	White fish fillets	600 g
1	Green pepper	1
2	Carrots	2
1	Small onion	1
1	Aubergine	1
7½ oz	Can of bamboo shoots	213 g
1	Egg	1
3 oz	Plain flour	75 g
1 oz	Cornflour	25 g
	Oil for deep frying	
8 oz	Shelled prawns	225 g
2 oz	Mushrooms	50 g
Tentsuyu sauce		
¼ pint	Chicken stock	150 ml
4 tbsp	Sake or sherry	4x15 ml
2 tbsp	Soy sauce	2x15 ml
6 inch	Piece of Japanese radish	15 cm

To make sauce, mix stock, sake or sherry and soy sauce in a pan. Bring to the boil, then pour into individual bowls and keep warm.

Remove skin from fish and cut into 1 inch (2.5 cm) wide strips. Deseed and slice pepper. Peel carrots and cut into matchsticks. Peel onion and cut into thick rings. Chop aubergine. Drain and chop bamboo shoots.

Beat egg with ¼ pint (150 ml) water. Sift flour and cornflour and gradually beat into egg to make a thin batter.

Heat oil in a saucepan to about 350°F (180°C). Transfer to metal fondue pot and place over flame in centre of table. Mix grated radish into sauce. Each person dips piece of fish or vegetable into batter, then fries and dips it in sauce.

Thai fish with sharp sauce

Overall timing 45 minutes

Freezing Not suitable

To serve 4

2x1 lb	Striped mullet	2x450 g
4 tbsp	Plain flour	4x15 ml
¼ pint	Oil	150 ml
1	Garlic clove	1
3 tbsp	Light soft brown sugar	3x15 ml
3 tbsp	White vinegar	3x15 ml
1 tbsp	Soy sauce	15 ml
½ inch	Piece of root ginger	12.5 mm
¼ pint	Water	150 ml
1 teasp	Cornflour	5 ml
6	Spring onions	6
2	Fresh green chillies	2
2	Fresh red chillies	2
	Salt and pepper	

Make three diagonal slashes in each side of each fish, then coat with flour. Heat oil in frying pan, add fish and fry gently for about 10 minutes on each side till tender and golden. Remove from pan, drain on kitchen paper and arrange on a warmed serving dish. Keep hot.

Pour off all but 1 tbsp (15 ml) oil from pan. Peel and crush garlic and fry in oil till golden. Stir in sugar, vinegar and soy sauce.

Peel and finely chop ginger and add to pan. Fry, stirring for 2 minutes, then add half the water. Blend cornflour with remaining water and add to pan. Bring to the boil, stirring constantly, and simmer for 3 minutes.

Meanwhile, trim and shred spring onions. Deseed chillies and cut into flower shapes. Scatter over the fish. Taste sauce and adjust seasoning. Pour over fish and serve.

Spicy fish with noodles

Overall timing 45 minutes

Freezing Not suitable

To serve 4

1 lb	Broad rice noodles	450 g
	Salt	
4 tbsp	Oil	4 x 15 ml
4 oz	Squid	125 g
2	Large onions	2
6	Fresh chillies	6
4	Garlic cloves	4
4 oz	Shelled prawns	125 g
4 oz	Bean sprouts	125 g
2 tbsp	Soy sauce	2 x 15 ml
1 tbsp	Oyster sauce	15 ml
4	Eggs	4

Cook the noodles in boiling salted water for about 5 minutes till tender. Drain and rinse under cold water. Add 1 teasp (5 ml) of the oil to prevent the noodles sticking together and reserve.

Prepare squid and cut into rings. Peel and slice the onions. Deseed and finely chop the chillies. Peel and crush garlic.

Heat half the remaining oil in frying pan and fry the onions, chillies and garlic for about 10 minutes till golden. Add the prawns and squid and stir-fry over a high heat for 2–3 minutes. Add the bean sprouts and a little salt and cook for 1 minute. Tip the mixture into a bowl and reserve.

Heat the remaining oil in pan and fry the reserved noodles for 2 minutes over a high heat, stirring in the soy sauce and oyster sauce. Return the fish and vegetable mixture to the pan and mix well.

Beat the eggs and pour over the noodles. Cook for 2–3 minutes, stirring till lightly set. Pile into a warmed serving dish and serve immediately with a side dish of chilli pickle.

Tahitian raw fish salad

Overall timing 2 hours 20 minutes

Freezing Not suitable

To serve 6

1½ lb	Firm white fish	700 g
4 tbsp	Lemon juice	4x15 ml
7 tbsp	Oil	7x15 ml
2 tbsp	Vinegar	2x15 ml
1 teasp	Made mustard	5 ml
	Salt and pepper	
2	Carrots	2
1	Green pepper	1
3	Tomatoes	3
¼	Fresh coconut	¼
4 tbsp	Mixed pickles	4x15 ml
8 oz	Can of palm hearts	227 g
2	Hard-boiled eggs	2

Cut the fish into very small cubes. Put into a bowl with the lemon juice and marinate for 2 hours in the refrigerator.

To make the dressing, beat together the oil, vinegar, mustard and seasoning in another bowl.

Peel and dice carrots. Deseed and slice pepper into thin strips. Blanch in boiling water for 2 minutes and drain. Cut tomatoes into wedges.

Coarsely grate coconut into salad bowl, reserving 1 tbsp (15 ml) for the garnish. Add drained fish, carrots, pepper, drained pickles and tomatoes. Drain palm hearts, slice and add to bowl. Pour dressing over and mix well.

Shell and slice hard-boiled eggs. Arrange on top of salad, sprinkle with reserved coconut and serve.

Malaysian fish casserole

Overall timing 45 minutes

Freezing Not suitable

To serve 4

1½ lb	Cod fillets	700 g
2 tbsp	Lemon juice	2x15 ml
3	Onions	3
4 tbsp	Milk	4x15 ml
6 tbsp	Plain flour	6x15 ml
1 oz	Butter	25 g
6 tbsp	Groundnut oil	6x15 ml
	Salt	
2 tbsp	Curry powder	2x15 ml
½ teasp	Ground ginger	2.5 ml
2 oz	Salted peanuts	50 g
¼ pint	Carton of single cream	150 ml

Skin cod fillets, cut into large pieces and arrange in a single layer on a plate. Sprinkle lemon juice over and marinate for 10 minutes.

Meanwhile, peel and thinly slice onions into rings. Toss them in milk and drain, then coat in half the flour. Heat butter and half the oil in a frying pan and fry onion rings for 3–5 minutes till golden. Drain on kitchen paper and keep hot.

Season remaining flour with salt and half the curry powder. Drain fish, reserving lemon juice, and coat with seasoned flour. Heat remaining oil in a flameproof casserole, add fish and fry for 3 minutes till tender and golden, turning occasionally. Remove from casserole and keep hot.

Add remaining curry powder and ginger to casserole and fry gently, stirring, for 2 minutes. Add peanuts and cook, stirring, till brown. Stir in reserved lemon juice, cream, onion rings and fish and cook gently for 5 minutes to heat through. Serve immediately with boiled rice.

Indonesian fish curry

Overall timing 40 minutes

Freezing Not suitable

To serve 4

1½ lb	Cod or coley fillets	700 g
	Salt and pepper	
2 tbsp	Plain flour	2x15 ml
1	Onion	1
1	Large cooking apple	1
1 tbsp	Lemon juice	15 ml
2 oz	Butter	50 g
2 tbsp	Oil	2x15 ml
2 tbsp	Curry powder	2x15 ml
1 pint	Stock	560 ml
2 tbsp	Sultanas	2x15 ml
2 tbsp	Cornflour	2x15 ml
2 oz	Split almonds	50 g

Cut fish into pieces, sprinkle with salt and coat with the flour. Peel and slice onion. Peel, core and slice apple and sprinkle with the lemon juice.

Heat the butter and oil in a flameproof casserole. Add curry powder and onion and fry for 5 minutes. Add fish and cook for a few minutes on all sides. Add apple slices and cook for 3 minutes.

Pour stock into casserole and add sultanas. Blend cornflour with a little stock or water and stir in. Bring to the boil and simmer for 10–15 minutes.

Add almonds and cook for a further 2 minutes. Taste and adjust seasoning and serve.

Japanese scampi and rice

Overall timing 35 minutes

Freezing Not suitable

To serve 4

8 oz	Shelled scampi	225 g
1	Egg	1
4 teasp	Plain flour	4x5 ml
¼ pint	Water	150 ml
	Salt and pepper	
	Oil for frying	
¼ pint	Stock	150 ml
2 tbsp	Soy sauce	2x15 ml
1 teasp	Sugar	5 ml
2 tbsp	Sweet sherry	2x15 ml

Cut lightly along back of each scampi. Mix egg, flour and water in a bowl with seasoning to make a smooth batter.

Heat 1 inch (2.5 cm) of oil in a frying pan. Dip the scampi in the batter, add to oil a few at a time and fry for 6–8 minutes, turning once, till golden and crisp. Remove with a draining spoon, drain on kitchen paper and keep hot.

Put the stock into a small saucepan with the soy sauce, sugar and sherry. Bring to the boil, stirring.

Arrange scampi on a bed of freshly boiled rice and pour over the sauce.

Thai fish moulds

Overall timing 1¼ hours

Freezing Not suitable

To serve 6

1 lb	Sole fillets	450 g
4 oz	White cabbage	125 g
1	Onion	1
1	Garlic clove	1
	Grated rind of 1 lemon	
	Chilli powder	
1 tbsp	Anchovy essence	15 ml
2 oz	Creamed coconut	50 g
2	Eggs	2
	Salt and pepper	
	Lemon wedges	

Preheat the oven to 375°F (190°C) Gas 5.

Remove skin from fish fillets, chop finely and put into a bowl. Trim and finely chop the cabbage. Peel and finely chop the onion. Peel and crush garlic. Add to fish with the grated lemon rind, a pinch of chilli powder and the anchovy essence.

Dilute the coconut with ¼ pint (150 ml) hot water, then strain. Beat the eggs and coconut milk together in a bowl. Season, then beat into fish.

Spoon the mixture into six greased moulds or ramekins. Cover each with foil and place in a roasting tin containing 1 inch (2.5 cm) hot water. Bake for about 40 minutes till the mixture is firm and a knife inserted into the centre comes out clean.

Turn the moulds out on to a warmed serving dish. Garnish with lemon wedges and serve immediately with hot buttered toast.

Lamb saté

Overall timing 1 hour plus marination

Freezing Not suitable

To serve 6

1½ lb	Boned leg of lamb	700 g
1	Garlic clove	1
4 tbsp	Soy sauce	4x15 ml
	Salt and pepper	
4 oz	Raw peanuts	125 g
4 tbsp	Groundnut oil	4x15 ml
1	Small onion	1
1 tbsp	Lemon juice	15 ml
½ teasp	Chilli powder	2.5 ml
¼ pint	Water	150 ml
1	Fresh chilli	1

Cut the lamb into small cubes. Peel and crush the garlic. Mix with 3 tbsp (3x15 ml) of the soy sauce and seasoning in a shallow dish. Add lamb, toss well and marinate for 3–4 hours, turning occasionally.

Meanwhile, make the peanut sauce. Gently fry the peanuts in half the oil for 10 minutes. Transfer to a blender or mortar. Peel and chop the onion and add with lemon juice, chilli powder and remaining soy sauce. Blend or pound the mixture till smooth.

Preheat the grill.

Heat the remaining oil in a saucepan and fry the peanut mixture for a few minutes. Gradually stir in the water and bring to the boil, stirring. Simmer the mixture till thick enough to coat the back of the spoon.

Thread the meat on to six skewers or saté sticks and grill for about 5 minutes on each side.

Meanwhile, deseed and slice the chilli. Pour the sauce into a warmed sauce boat, decorate with the chilli and serve with the lamb skewers.

Sesame and spinach salad

Overall timing 25 minutes plus chilling

Freezing Not suitable

To serve 6

2 lb	Fresh spinach	900 g
	Salt and pepper	
2 tbsp	Sesame seeds	2x15 ml
2 teasp	Oil	2x5 ml
2 tbsp	Soy sauce	2x15 ml

Put the spinach into a saucepan with only the water that clings to it after washing and a little salt. Bring to the boil, cover and simmer for 5 minutes. Drain thoroughly and put into a serving dish. Leave to cool completely.

Put the sesame seeds into a small saucepan and dry fry till golden. Grind lightly. Add the oil and soy sauce and season to taste. Pour over the spinach and chill for 30 minutes.

Toss lightly before serving with fried or grilled meats or fish.

Indonesian apple rice

Overall timing 20 minutes

Freezing Not suitable

To serve 4

9 oz	Rice	250 g
	Salt	
2	Dessert apples	2
1	Onion	1
2 tbsp	Oil	2x15 ml
3 tbsp	Sultanas	3x15 ml
2 tbsp	Flaked almonds	2x15 ml
2 oz	Mushrooms	50 g
2 oz	Black olives	50 g
2 oz	Stuffed green olives	50 g
2 teasp	Brown sugar	2x5 ml
1 tbsp	Curry powder	15 ml
	Slices of apple	

Cook the rice in boiling salted water for 15 minutes till tender.

Meanwhile, core and chop apples. Peel and chop onion. Heat oil in another saucepan. Add apples and onion and cook till transparent, stirring occasionally to prevent sticking.

Stir in the sultanas, almonds, sliced mushrooms and olives and cook for a few minutes. Add a pinch of salt, the sugar and curry powder. Mix well and cook for 3–4 minutes.

Remove rice from heat and drain well, if necessary. Combine with the curried mixture, garnish with slices of apple and serve.

Singapore coconut pudding

Overall timing 45 minutes plus 30 minutes soaking

Freezing Not suitable

To serve 4

3 oz	Desiccated coconut	75 g
4 fl oz	Boiling water	120 ml
8 oz	Caster sugar	225 g
3	Eggs	3
	Pinch of salt	
4 tbsp	Grated fresh coconut	4x15 ml

Put desiccated coconut in a bowl and pour over boiling water. Soak for 30 minutes, then pour through muslin or a fine sieve into a jug. Squeeze out liquid from coconut. Discard coconut.

Preheat the oven to 350°F (180°C) Gas 4.

Beat the sugar, eggs and salt till thick and foamy. Gradually add reserved coconut liquid.

Turn the mixture into a lightly greased 1 pint (560 ml) mould or four ovenproof dishes and place in roasting tin half-filled with hot water. Bake for 30 minutes.

Allow to cool, then invert over a serving plate to turn out. Chill until ready to serve, sprinkled with grated fresh coconut.

Guacamole with taco chips

Overall timing 45 minutes

Freezing Suitable

To serve 8

1 oz	Lard	25 g
10 oz	Masa harina (precooked maizemeal)	275 g
4 oz	Plain flour	125 g
1 pint	Warm water	560 ml
	Oil for frying	
Guacamole		
2	Ripe avocados	2
4 tbsp	Lemon juice	4 x 15 ml
½ teasp	Onion salt	2.5 ml
1	Tomato	1
	Paprika	

First, make the guacamole. Remove flesh from avocados and mash with lemon juice and onion salt. Peel and chop tomato and add with a pinch of paprika. Cover and set aside.

Grease a griddle or heavy-based frying pan with a little of the lard and place on moderate heat.

Put masa harina and flour in a bowl and gradually stir in the water. Mix well until dough is soft and pliable and leaves the sides of the bowl. Divide dough into 36 and shape into balls.

Place balls between sheets of greaseproof paper and press between two wooden boards to make thin pancakes. Fry tortillas, one at a time, for 2 minutes till sides lift a little, then turn over and cook other side for 2 minutes, pressing with the flat of a knife so tortilla puffs slightly. Keep warm while remaining tortillas are fried, regreasing the griddle or pan as required.

Heat oil in deep fryer to 360°F (180°C). Cut each tortilla into eight pieces, then deep fry for 2 minutes till golden brown. Drain on kitchen paper and serve with guacamole.

Mexican enchiladas

Overall timing 45 minutes

Freezing Not suitable

To serve 6

2½ lb	Ripe tomatoes	1.35 kg
4	Medium onions	4
3	Fresh green chillies	3
3 tbsp	Oil	3x15 ml
2 tbsp	Tomato purée	2x15 ml
¼ pint	Chicken stock	150 ml
¼ teasp	Sugar	1.25 ml
	Salt and pepper	
1 tbsp	Chopped fresh coriander	15 ml
1 tbsp	Lemon or lime juice	15 ml
18	Tortillas (see opposite)	18
4 oz	Cheese	125 g

Blanch, peel and quarter 2 lb (900 g) tomatoes, then sieve to a purée. Peel and finely chop two onions. Deseed and slice one chilli.

Heat 1 tbsp (15 ml) oil in a saucepan and fry chopped onions till golden. Stir in tomatoes, tomato purée, stock, sliced chilli, sugar and seasoning. Simmer till thick.

Meanwhile, make the salcita. Chop the remaining tomatoes. Peel and finely chop one onion. Deseed and thinly slice remaining chillies. Mix all with the coriander, lemon or lime juice and seasoning. Set aside.

Heat remaining oil in a frying pan. Fry tortillas, turning once, till golden brown. Drain on kitchen paper. Keep warm.

Peel and thinly slice remaining onion and mix lightly with grated cheese. Reserve one-third to garnish.

Taste tomato sauce and adjust seasoning. Dip tortillas, one at a time, into sauce to moisten them. Sprinkle cheese and onion mixture over centre of each tortilla and roll up. Arrange, join down, in layers, on a warmed serving dish. Pour over remaining sauce and sprinkle with the reserved cheese and onion mixture. Serve immediately with the salcita.

Santo Domingo soup

Overall timing 50 minutes

Freezing Suitable

To serve 6

2 lb	Mixed fish	900 g
2	Onions	2
1	Garlic clove	1
2	Tomatoes	2
3	Medium potatoes	3
8 oz	White cabbage	225 g
2	Green peppers	2
6 tbsp	Oil	6x15 ml
4 oz	Long grain rice	125 g
1¾ pints	Fish stock or water	1 litre
1 tbsp	Tomato purée	15 ml
8 oz	Shelled prawns	225 g
¼ teasp	Dried oregano	1.25 ml
	Salt and pepper	

Remove skin and bones from fish and cut into bite-size pieces. Peel and chop onions and garlic. Blanch, peel and chop tomatoes. Peel potatoes and cut into small chunks. Shred cabbage. Deseed and dice peppers.

Heat the oil in a flameproof casserole and fry the onions and garlic till golden. Add the rice, then the fish and fry for 5 minutes, stirring all the time. Add prepared vegetables and stock or water. Bring to the boil.

Mix tomato purée with a little hot water and stir into the casserole. Cook for 15 minutes. Add prawns, oregano and seasoning and cook for a further 10 minutes.

West Indian crab

Overall timing 45 minutes

Freezing Not suitable

To serve 6

2	Onions	2
1½ lb	Medium potatoes	700 g
12 oz	Okra	350 g
2 oz	Butter	50 g
1 teasp	Chilli powder	5 ml
14 oz	Can of tomatoes	397 g
1	Bay leaf	1
	Sprig of thyme	
½ pint	Light stock	300 ml
2x6 oz	Cans of crabmeat	2x170 g
	Salt and pepper	
1 tbsp	Chopped parsley	15 ml

Peel and thinly slice the onions. Peel the potatoes and cut into thick slices. Trim the okra. Melt the butter in a flameproof casserole and fry the onions till transparent. Add the okra, potatoes and chilli powder and fry, stirring, for 5 minutes.

Add the tomatoes and their juice, bay leaf, thyme and stock. Bring to the boil, cover and simmer for 10 minutes till potatoes are tender.

Drain the crabmeat and flake into large pieces. Add to the casserole, stirring carefully so that the pieces of crab don't disintegrate. Simmer gently for 5 minutes. Remove bay leaf and thyme and adjust seasoning.

Arrange in warmed serving dish, sprinkle with parsley and serve immediately with boiled rice.

Jamaican cod fritters

Overall timing 50 minutes

Freezing Not suitable

To serve 4

4 oz	Plain flour	125 g
1½ teasp	Salt	7.5 ml
1	Egg	1
1 tbsp	Oil	15 ml
4 fl oz	Milk	120 ml
2	Onions	2
8 oz	Cod fillets	225 g
	Salt and pepper	
1	Garlic clove	1
1	Fresh red chilli	1
1 tbsp	Chopped parsley	15 ml
	Oil for frying	
2	Egg whites	2
1	Lime or lemon	1

Sift flour and salt into a bowl and make a well in the centre. Stir in whole egg and oil, then gradually add milk and beat till batter is smooth.

Peel and quarter one of the onions. Put into a pan with cod, 1 pint (560 ml) water and seasoning. Bring to the boil, cover and simmer for 10 minutes. Drain and mash cod.

Peel and chop remaining onion and garlic. Deseed and slice chilli. Mix mashed cod, onion, garlic, chilli and chopped parsley into the batter.

Heat oil in deep-fryer to 360°F (180°C). Whisk egg whites till stiff, then carefully fold into batter. Scoop out a little batter in a spoon and shape by placing a second spoon on top. Put into the hot oil and cook, in batches, for 1–2 minutes till golden all over. Drain on kitchen paper. Serve hot with buttered fingers of toast and wedges of lime or lemon.

Plantain chips

Overall timing 35 minutes plus soaking

Freezing Not suitable

To serve 4

1	Large plantain	1
4 teasp	Salt	4x5 ml
2 pints	Water	1.1 litre
6 tbsp	Oil	6x15 ml
2	Limes	2

Peel the plantain (a Caribbean vegetable that resembles a banana) and cut diagonally into ½ inch (12.5 mm) slices. Put three-quarters of the salt into a bowl with the water and stir till salt dissolves. Add plantain slices and leave to soak for 45 minutes.

Drain slices thoroughly and pat dry. Heat the oil in a large frying pan. Add plantain slices and fry very gently without browning for 10 minutes or until just tender. Remove from pan with a draining spoon, reserving oil. Spread out plantain slices between two sheets of greased greaseproof paper. Using a rolling-pin, flatten slices until ¼ inch (6 mm) thick.

Squeeze juice from limes into a bowl and add remaining 1 teasp (5 ml) salt. Reheat oil in frying pan. Dip each plantain slice into lime mixture, then fry for 3 minutes on each side over a high heat until crusty and golden. Remove from pan with draining spoon and drain on kitchen paper. Serve hot, sprinkled with salt.

Chilli con carne

Overall timing 3¼ hours plus overnight soaking

Freezing Suitable

To serve 4-6

8 oz	**Dried brown or red beans**	225 g
1¾ pints	**Water**	1 litre
2 lb	**Braising steak**	900 g
1	**Onion**	1
1 tbsp	**Pork dripping or olive oil**	15 ml
1 oz	**Butter**	25 g
	Salt and pepper	
1 teasp	**Chilli powder**	5 ml
1 tbsp	**Sweet paprika**	15 ml
8 oz	**Canned tomatoes**	225 g
2 teasp	**Cornflour (optional)**	2x5 ml

Soak beans in water overnight. The next day, place water and beans in saucepan, cover and cook gently for 1½ hours.

Cut the beef into 1 inch (2.5 cm) cubes. Peel and chop onion. Heat the dripping or oil and butter in frying pan. Add the beef. Cook till brown, then add the onion and cook till transparent.

Mix the meat and onion in with the cooked beans and season with salt, pepper, chilli powder and paprika. Cover and cook gently for 1 hour.

Add the drained tomatoes, cover and cook for 30 minutes more. Adjust seasoning. If you wish to thicken the sauce, blend the cornflour with a little water and add it to the mixture. Cook for a few minutes, then serve from the cooking pot with plain boiled rice or chunks of wholemeal bread and a crisp green salad.

Haitian pork with sauce ti-malice

Overall timing 1¼ hours plus overnight marination

Freezing Not suitable

To serve 6–8

3 lb	Lean pork	1.4 kg
1	Large onion	1
1	Green pepper	1
1	Garlic clove	1
3	Seville oranges	3
	Salt and pepper	
½ pint	Light stock	300 ml
4 tbsp	Oil	4x15 ml
Sauce ti-malice		
2	Large onions	2
1	Garlic clove	1
1	Red pepper	1
4	Fresh green chillies	4
2	Limes	2
1 tbsp	Oil	15 ml
	Salt and pepper	
5 tbsp	Tomato purée	5x15 ml

To make sauce, peel and thinly slice onions. Peel and crush garlic. Deseed and slice red pepper and chillies. Squeeze juice from limes. Put all into pan with oil and seasoning. Cook for 10 minutes. Add tomato purée and seasoning, then cool and chill overnight.

Cut pork into 2 inch (5 cm) cubes and place in a large bowl. Peel and finely chop onion. Deseed and slice green pepper. Peel and crush garlic. Squeeze juice from oranges. Add all to pork with seasoning. Cover and marinate in refrigerator overnight.

Next day, put pork and marinade into flameproof casserole and add stock. Cover and simmer for 1 hour till pork is just tender.

Drain pork thoroughly. Heat oil in clean casserole and fry pork, a little at a time, till crisp and golden. Serve hot, with cold sauce.

West Indian peanut pie

Overall timing 1¼ hours

Freezing Not suitable

To serve 6–8

Pastry		
4 oz	Self-raising flour	125 g
½ teasp	Salt	2.5 ml
2 tbsp	Caster sugar	2x15 ml
2 oz	Softened butter	50 g
1	Egg yolk	1
2 tbsp	Milk	2x15 ml
Filling		
4 oz	Roasted unsalted peanuts	125 g
1	Egg	1
3 oz	Sugar	75 g
4 oz	Golden syrup	125 g
½ teasp	Vanilla essence	2.5 ml

Preheat the oven to 350°F (180°C) Gas 4.

To make pastry, sift flour, salt and sugar into a bowl. Rub in the butter. Add egg yolk and gradually mix in enough milk to bind to a soft dough. Roll out dough and use to line an 8 inch (20 cm) fluted flan ring.

To make filling, preheat the grill. Remove the shells from the peanuts. Place nuts on a baking tray and grill them for 2 minutes, shaking the tray so they brown lightly all over. Remove and allow to cool.

Whisk the egg and sugar in a bowl till light and frothy. Add syrup and continue to beat till thick. Stir in the peanuts and vanilla essence.

Pour the peanut mixture into the flan ring and bake for 30 minutes. Cover with foil and bake for a further 5–10 minutes. Lift off the foil, leave the pie till almost cool, then remove from tin.

Individual coconut soufflés

Overall timing 45 minutes

Freezing Not suitable

To serve 8

½ pint	Milk	300 ml
5 tbsp	Caster sugar	5x15 ml
2 tbsp	Plain flour	2x15 ml
2 oz	Butter	50 g
4	Eggs	4
4 oz	Desiccated coconut	125 g
1 tbsp	Icing sugar	15 ml

Whisk 4 tbsp (4x15 ml) of the milk with 3 tbsp (3x15 ml) of the caster sugar and the flour. Bring the remaining milk to the boil in a saucepan. Add 2 tbsp (2x15 ml) of the boiling milk to the sugar mixture and whisk in well, then add to the milk in the pan, whisking vigorously all the time. Simmer gently till thickened, then cover, remove from heat and leave to cool for 15 minutes.

Preheat the oven to 375°F (190°C) Gas 5. Grease eight ovenproof moulds or ramekins with the butter and sprinkle with 1 tbsp (15 ml) of the sugar.

Separate the eggs. Add the yolks to the sauce with the coconut, whisking all the time. In a large bowl, whisk the egg whites till they hold stiff peaks, gradually adding the remaining sugar. Fold into the egg yolk mixture.

Three-quarters fill the moulds or ramekins with the mixture and sprinkle with icing sugar. Place on baking tray and bake for 20 minutes. Serve hot.

Avocado and banana fool

Overall timing 20 minutes plus chilling

Freezing Suitable

To serve 6

2	Ripe avocados	2
3	Large bananas	3
3 tbsp	Lemon juice	3x15 ml
2 tbsp	White rum	2x15 ml
6 tbsp	Light soft brown sugar	6x15 ml
$\frac{1}{4}$ pint	Carton of double cream	150 ml
	Green food colouring (optional)	

Cut the avocados in half and discard the stones. Scoop out the flesh and put into a blender. Peel the bananas and add to the blender with the lemon juice, rum and sugar. Blend till smooth. Transfer to a large bowl.

Whip the cream till soft peaks form, then fold into the avocado mixture with a metal spoon, adding a few drops of green food colouring, if liked. Divide between individual dishes and chill for at least 2 hours before serving.

Stewed pumpkin

Overall timing 1½ hours plus chilling

Freezing Suitable

To serve 6–8

2	Oranges	2
1¼ pints	Water	700 ml
1¼ lb	Granulated sugar	600 g
3 inch	Cinnamon stick	7.5 cm
2 lb	Pumpkin	900 g

Peel the oranges and finely shred the rind. Squeeze juice into a saucepan. Add orange rind, water, sugar and cinnamon and stir over a low heat till the sugar dissolves. Bring to the boil and simmer for about 30 minutes till the orange rind is tender.

Peel the pumpkin, discard the seeds and fibrous centre and cut the flesh into wide strips. Add to the syrup with a few of the seeds (scraped to remove fibres) and bring back to the boil. Simmer for about 30 minutes till the pumpkin is soft.

Remove from the heat and allow to cool completely. Transfer to a serving dish and chill for 3–4 hours. Serve cold with pouring cream and crisp biscuits as a dessert.

The Arab World

Saudi Arabian soup

Overall timing 1 hour

Freezing Suitable

To serve 6

8 oz	Carrots	225 g
2 tbsp	Oil	2x15 ml
12 oz	Boned chicken	350 g
2½ pints	Home-made chicken stock	1.5 litres
	Salt and pepper	
8 oz	Courgettes	225 g
8 oz	Green beans	225 g

Peel the carrots and cut into ½ inch (12.5 mm) slices. Heat the oil in a saucepan, add the carrots and fry over a moderate heat for 10 minutes till beginning to brown.

Meanwhile, cut the chicken into neat pieces, discarding the skin. Add to the pan. Fry, stirring, for 5 minutes. Add the stock and seasoning and bring to the boil. Cover and simmer for 30 minutes.

Cut the courgettes into ½ inch (12.5 mm) slices. Top and tail the beans and cut in half lengthways. Add the vegetables to the soup and simmer for a further 10 minutes. Adjust the seasoning and pour into a warmed serving dish. Serve immediately with hot pitta bread.

Falafel

Overall timing 20 minutes plus standing

Freezing Not suitable

Makes 20

12 oz	Cooked chickpeas	350 g
1	Medium onion	1
1 oz	Fresh breadcrumbs	25 g
2 tbsp	Chopped parsley	2x15 ml
1 teasp	Ground cumin	5 ml
1 teasp	Ground coriander	5 ml
	Salt	
	Cayenne pepper	
	Oil for frying	

Purée the chickpeas in a blender or pound to a paste in a mortar. Put into a bowl.

Peel and finely chop onion and add to chickpeas with the breadcrumbs. Stir in 2 tbsp (2x15 ml) water. Add parsley, spices, salt and cayenne. Mix well and leave to stand for 1 hour.

Taste the mixture and adjust the seasoning. Roll into 1 inch (2.5 cm) balls between floured hands. Heat oil in a deep-fryer to 360°F (180°C) and fry the balls, a few at a time, for about 3 minutes till golden. Drain thoroughly on kitchen paper, then spike with cocktail sticks and serve with fingers of grilled pitta bread and wedges or thinly-cut slices of lemon.

Moroccan cold tuna

Overall timing 1¼ hours plus marination and chilling

Freezing Not suitable

To serve 6–8

6 tbsp	Oil	6x15 ml
2 teasp	Harissa sauce	2x5 ml
1 teasp	Ground cumin	5 ml
	Salt and pepper	
2 lb	Tuna steak	900 g
3	Large onions	3
1 teasp	Mixed spice	5 ml
1 teasp	Ground cinnamon	5 ml
¼ pint	Red wine vinegar	150 ml
1 tbsp	Clear honey	15 ml
4 oz	Seedless raisins	125 g
1	Lemon	1

Put 4 tbsp (4x15 ml) of the oil into a shallow dish and stir in half the harissa, the cumin and a large pinch of salt. Mix well, add the tuna and turn in the mixture till coated. Cover and marinate in the refrigerator for 1 hour.

Drain tuna. Heat the remaining oil in a flameproof casserole, add the tuna and fry for 5 minutes each side. Remove the tuna and reserve. Peel and slice the onions. Add to the pan and fry till transparent. Add the remaining harissa, the spices and pepper and stir over a low heat for 3 minutes. Add vinegar, honey and raisins and boil for 5 minutes till the liquid has reduced by one-third.

Return the tuna to the pan, cover and simmer for about 40 minutes till tender. Remove from the heat and leave to cool, then chill for 3–4 hours.

Peel and thinly slice the lemon. Use to garnish the tuna and serve immediately with a tossed green salad.

Cheese boureks

Overall timing 1 hour

Freezing Suitable: bake from frozen in 400°F (200°C) Gas 6 oven for 20 minutes

To serve 4–6

Paste		
3 tbsp	Lukewarm water	3x15 ml
1 teasp	Dried yeast	5 ml
½ teasp	Caster sugar	2.5 ml
3 oz	Fine maizemeal	75 g
6 oz	Plain flour	175 g
2	Eggs	2
4 teasp	Olive oil	4x5 ml
	Salt	
Filling		
8 oz	Cottage cheese	225 g
½ pint	White sauce	300 ml
2 tbsp	Chopped parsley	2x15 ml
	Salt and pepper	
1	Egg	1
1 oz	Butter	25 g

Mix water, yeast and sugar and leave in warm place till frothy.

Preheat the oven to 400°F (200°C) Gas 6. Mix maizemeal and flour on a board and make a well in the centre. Pour in the yeast mixture, eggs, oil and a pinch of salt. Mix with a fork, gradually drawing dry ingredients into liquid. Knead dough till smooth, then roll out thinly. Stamp out sixteen 4 inch (10 cm) rounds.

Mix the cheese with the white sauce, parsley and seasoning. Divide cheese mixture between dough rounds. Lightly beat the egg and brush around the edges. Fold rounds over to enclose filling, pressing edges together to seal.

Arrange boureks in greased ovenproof dish. Melt the butter and brush over. Bake for 25 minutes. Serve hot with a selection of salads.

Ful medames with hamine eggs

Overall timing 5¼ hours plus overnight soaking

Freezing Not suitable

To serve 6

1 lb	Ful medames (dried brown beans)	450 g
4	Eggs	4
4	Medium brown-skinned onions	4
2	Garlic cloves	2
6 tbsp	Olive oil	6x15 ml
3 tbsp	Chopped parsley	3x15 ml
	Salt and pepper	
	Lemon wedges	
	Flat-leaf parsley	

Soak beans in cold water overnight.

The next day, place unshelled eggs and all layers of onion skins in a large saucepan. Cover with cold water, bring to the boil, cover, and simmer as gently as possible for 5 hours, topping up with boiling water as necessary. The dye from the onion skins turns the egg shells a dark brown, and the egg white pale beige.

After the eggs have been cooking for 2½ hours, drain the beans. Place in a large saucepan and cover with fresh cold water. Bring to the boil, cover and simmer for about 2½ hours till tender, but not overcooked.

Drain the beans well. Peel and crush garlic and add to beans with the olive oil, chopped parsley and seasoning. Toss lightly till the beans are evenly coated with the dressing. Pile the beans on to a serving dish.

Shell the eggs and cut into quarters lengthways. Garnish the beans with the eggs, lemon wedges and parsley. Or, serve in soup bowls with the halved egg on top and pass round extra oil, parsley and seasoning.

Egyptian lamb with okra

Overall timing 1¼ hours

Freezing Not suitable

To serve 6

2 lb	Lean lamb	900 g
1 lb	Onions	450 g
2	Garlic cloves	2
4 tbsp	Oil	4x15 ml
½ teasp	Ground coriander	2.5 ml
1 lb	Tomatoes	450 g
½ pint	Stock	300 ml
	Salt and pepper	
1 lb	Okra	450 g
1 oz	Butter	25 g
2 tbsp	Lemon juice	2x15 ml

Cut lamb into 1 inch (2.5 cm) chunks. Peel and chop the onions. Peel and crush garlic. Heat half the oil in a saucepan and add the onions and garlic. Fry until just beginning to brown.

Add coriander and lamb and brown on all sides. Blanch, peel and chop tomatoes. Add to pan with stock and seasoning. Cover and simmer for about 1 hour.

Meanwhile, trim okra. Cook in boiling salted water for 5 minutes. Drain well and dry. Heat remaining oil and the butter in a large frying pan and fry the okra, without browning, until tender. Add the lemon juice and season to taste. Garnish the lamb stew with the okra.

Persian beef soup

Overall timing 45 minutes

Freezing Not suitable

To serve 6

1 lb	Minced beef	450 g
1 tbsp	Lemon juice	15 ml
1	Egg	1
	Salt and pepper	
8	Spring onions	8
2 oz	Butter	50 g
3 oz	Long grain rice	75 g
$\frac{3}{4}$ pint	Natural yogurt	400 ml
8 oz	Cooked chickpeas	225 g
4 tbsp	Olive oil	4x15 ml
1 tbsp	Dried mint	5 ml

Pound beef to a paste with lemon juice, egg and seasoning. Shape with floured hands into small balls.

Trim onions and cut into 2 inch (5 cm) lengths. Melt butter in saucepan and fry onions gently for 3 minutes. Add rice and cook for 1 minute, stirring. Stir in yogurt, chickpeas, 2 pints (1.1 litres) water and salt. Bring to the boil, cover and simmer for 15 minutes.

Meanwhile, heat oil in frying pan and brown meatballs on all sides. Drain and add to soup. Simmer for a further 5 minutes till rice is tender. Pour into serving dish and sprinkle with mint.

Lebanese yogurt dip

Overall timing 20 minutes plus overnight draining

Freezing Not suitable

To serve 4

1$\frac{1}{2}$ teasp	Salt	7.5 ml
1$\frac{1}{2}$ pints	Natural yogurt	850 ml
2 teasp	Olive oil	2x5 ml
1 teasp	Dried mint	5 ml
	Cucumber slices	
	Fresh mint leaves	
	Black olive	

Wring a piece of muslin out in cold water and use to line a colander, leaving the corners hanging over the edge. Stir the salt into the yogurt and pour it into the colander. Lift the corners of the muslin and tie them together. Hang the yogurt over a bowl and leave to drain overnight.

Next day, spoon the curds on to a serving dish. Mix the oil and dried mint together and sprinkle on top. Garnish with cucumber slices, fresh mint and a black olive and serve immediately with hot pitta bread and pickles.

Iranian omelette

Overall timing 30 minutes

Freezing Not suitable

To serve 4

1	Large onion	1
9 oz	Aubergines	250 g
4 fl oz	Oil	120 ml
1 teasp	Madras curry powder	5 ml
	Salt and pepper	
4	Large eggs	4

Peel and slice onion. Dice aubergines. Heat a little oil in a saucepan. Cook onion till golden brown, then remove from pan.

Put a little more oil into pan and heat. Add aubergines and brown on all sides. Add curry powder and seasoning. Return onions to pan and cook till aubergines are tender. Remove from heat and cool.

Lightly beat eggs and mix carefully into aubergine mixture. Heat remaining oil in a large frying pan. Pour in egg and aubergine mixture and cook for about 5 minutes, shaking pan to prevent omelette sticking. Cut omelette into sections and turn pieces over one at a time to brown other sides.

Kufta

Overall timing 20 minutes plus standing

Freezing Suitable: fry from frozen, allowing 20 minutes

To serve 4-6

3	Onions	3
1 lb	Minced lamb	450 g
1 lb	Minced beef	450 g
4	Eggs	4
2 oz	Fresh breadcrumbs	50 g
	Cayenne pepper	
$\frac{1}{2}$ teasp	Dried oregano	2.5 ml
3 tbsp	Chopped parsley	3x15 ml
$\frac{1}{4}$ pint	Milk	150 ml
	Salt and pepper	
3 tbsp	Plain flour	3x15 ml
2 oz	Dried breadcrumbs	50 g
1 tbsp	Oil	15 ml
2 oz	Butter	50 g

Peel and finely chop onions. Mix with lamb, beef, two eggs, fresh breadcrumbs, a pinch of cayenne pepper, herbs, milk and seasoning. Leave to stand for 1 hour.

Shape mixture into patties and coat with flour. Beat remaining eggs. Dip patties into eggs, then dried breadcrumbs. Heat oil and butter in frying pan and fry kufta for 5 minutes on each side till crisp and brown.

Moroccan lamb with couscous

Overall timing 1 hour

Freezing Not suitable

To serve 4

8 oz	Precooked couscous	225 g
2 lb	Boned shoulder of lamb	900 g
2	Garlic cloves	2
4 tbsp	Oil	4x15 ml
	Salt	
1 tbsp	Paprika	15 ml
$\frac{1}{2}$ pint	Stock	300 ml
$\frac{1}{2}$ teasp	Dried chervil	2.5 ml
1 tbsp	Chopped parsley	15 ml
$\frac{1}{4}$ teasp	Cayenne	1.25 ml
1 oz	Butter	25 g
	Sprigs of parsley	

Cook the couscous according to the packet instructions.

Cut lamb into cubes. Peel and crush garlic. Heat oil in frying pan and add garlic and meat. Brown on all sides. Season with salt and paprika, then add stock, chervil, chopped parsley and cayenne. Cover and simmer for 45 minutes till tender. Taste and adjust seasoning if necessary.

Melt the butter in a saucepan. Add the cooked couscous and stir until well coated. Pile couscous on to a warmed serving plate, arrange meat on top and serve garnished with parsley sprigs.

Dolmas

Overall timing 1¼ hours

Freezing Not suitable

To serve 4

1	White cabbage	1
3 oz	Long grain rice	75 g
1	Small onion	1
6 tbsp	Oil	6x15 ml
8 oz	Minced beef	225 g
	Salt and pepper	
¼ teasp	Grated nutmeg	1.25 ml
1 teasp	Dried oregano	5 ml
8 fl oz	Stock	220 ml
1 oz	Butter	25 g
1 tbsp	Plain flour	15 ml
1	Egg	1
2	Egg yolks	2
6 tbsp	Lemon juice	6x15 ml
¾ pint	White sauce	400 ml

Remove core from cabbage and cook in boiling water for 5 minutes. Drain and cool, then peel away 16–20 leaves. Add rice to same pan of boiling water and cook till tender. Drain.

Peel and chop onion. Heat 4 tbsp (4x15 ml) oil in a frying pan and cook onion till transparent. Add mince, salt, pepper, nutmeg and oregano. Cook for 5–8 minutes. Cool, then mix in rice.

Place a little stuffing on each cabbage leaf. Fold in sides and roll into right parcels. Heat rest of oil in flameproof casserole. Pack cabbage rolls tightly in casserole and pour in stock. Cut leftover cabbage heart in two and place on top. Cover and simmer gently for 40 minutes.

Transfer cabbage rolls to warmed serving dish. Pour cooking liquor into a measuring jug and make up to 8 fl oz (220 ml) with water if necessary.

Melt butter in saucepan, then stir in flour and cooking liquor and simmer until thickened. Beat egg and egg yolks with lemon juice till foamy. Add to pan off heat. Return to a gentle heat. Don't allow sauce to boil. Stir in white sauce and heat. Pour sauce over rolls.

Lamb and spinach tajin

Overall timing 3 hours plus overnight soaking

Freezing Not suitable

To serve 4

4 oz	Dried borlotti beans	125 g
1 lb	Boned shoulder of lamb	450 g
½ teasp	Chilli powder	2.5 ml
1	Onion	1
4 tbsp	Olive oil	4x15 ml
2 tbsp	Tomato purée	2x15 ml
1 pint	Water	560 ml
	Salt and pepper	
2 oz	Butter	50 g
8 oz	Fresh spinach	225 g
3 tbsp	Grated Parmesan cheese	3x15 ml
4 tbsp	Fresh breadcrumbs	4x15 ml
2	Eggs	2

Soak the beans in cold water overnight.

Drain beans, place in saucepan and cover with fresh cold water. Bring to the boil and simmer for 30 minutes. Drain.

Preheat the oven to 325°F (170°C) Gas 3.

Cut meat into cubes. Sprinkle with chilli powder. Peel and chop onion. Heat oil in flameproof casserole. Add meat and onion and fry over high heat for 5 minutes till meat is browned. Add tomato purée, beans and water. Bring to the boil, stirring. Season, cover and bake in the oven for 1½ hours.

Meanwhile, melt butter in frying pan, add spinach and cook over medium heat for 10 minutes, stirring.

Stir spinach, cheese and breadcrumbs into the bean mixture. Adjust seasoning. Beat eggs and stir into mixture. Bake for a further 30 minutes.

Egyptian fruit salad

Overall timing 15 minutes plus 48 hours soaking

Freezing Not suitable

To serve 6

8 oz	Dried apricots	225 g
4 oz	Stoned prunes	125 g
2 oz	Seedless raisins	50 g
4 oz	Dried figs	125 g
2 oz	Flaked almonds	50 g
1 oz	Pistachio nuts	25 g
½ pint	Water	300 ml
1 oz	Caster sugar	25 g
1 tbsp	Orange flower water	15 ml
2 teasp	Rose flower water	2x5 ml

Place the dried fruit in a shallow dish, halving the figs if very large. Sprinkle nuts over. Mix together the water, sugar and flower waters. Pour over fruit.

Chill for 48 hours, stirring occasionally. Serve very cold with crisp biscuits or single cream. If liked, place the serving dish in another dish filled with ice cubes and fresh grapes.

Mulligatawny soup

Overall timing 2½ hours

Freezing Not suitable

To serve 6

1	Carrot	1
1	Leek	1
	Bouquet garni	
	Strip of lemon rind	
2½ lb	Boiling chicken	1.1 kg
3 pints	Water	1.7 litres
1	Large onion	1
1 oz	Butter or ghee	25 g
1 tbsp	Mild curry powder	15 ml
1 teasp	Ground turmeric	5 ml
3 tbsp	Plain flour	3x15 ml
3 oz	Long grain rice	75 g
	Salt	
4 tbsp	Natural yogurt	4x15 ml

Peel and chop the carrot. Trim and chop the leek. Place in a large saucepan with bouquet garni and lemon rind. Add the chicken with the water. Bring to the boil, skim off any scum, cover and simmer for 1½ hours.

Peel and chop the onion. Melt the fat in a flameproof casserole, add onion and fry gently till transparent. Mix the curry powder, turmeric and flour in a small bowl and gradually add ¼ pint (150 ml) cold water. Pour into the casserole and bring to the boil, stirring constantly. Remove from heat.

Lift the chicken out of the stock. Strain the stock into the curry sauce a little at a time. Bring to the boil, stirring. Stir in the rice and salt, cover and simmer for 15 minutes.

Meanwhile, cut the chicken into neat pieces, discarding the skin and bones. Add to the soup and simmer for a further 3–5 minutes till the rice is tender. Taste and adjust the seasoning. Put the yogurt into a tureen, pour the soup on to it and serve immediately.

Curried prawns

Overall timing 1 hour

Freezing Not suitable

To serve 4

2 oz	Butter or ghee	50 g
1½ lb	Raw prawns	700 g
½ pint	Water	300 ml
1	Onion	1
½ teasp	Ground turmeric	2.5 ml
2 tbsp	Ground coriander	2x15 ml
¼ teasp	Cayenne pepper	1.25 ml
	Salt and pepper	
¼ pint	Natural yogurt	150 ml

Melt half the fat in a saucepan and fry the prawns till bright pink. Lift out of the pan and remove the shells. Reserve the prawns and return the shells to the pan. Add the water, bring to the boil, cover and simmer the stock for 15 minutes.

Meanwhile, peel and thinly slice the onion. Melt the remaining fat in a flameproof casserole and fry the onion gently till golden brown. Add the prawns and fry for 2 minutes.

Mix the turmeric, coriander, cayenne pepper and seasoning in a bowl. Sprinkle over the prawns and fry gently for 2 more minutes. Strain the stock over the prawns and bring to the boil. Stir in the yogurt and simmer for 10 minutes. Adjust the seasoning and serve with plain boiled rice.

Fish with tamarind

Overall timing 1¼ hours plus marination

Freezing Not suitable

To serve 4

4	White fish steaks	4
6 tbsp	Plain flour	6x15 ml
3	Garlic cloves	3
½ teasp	Ground turmeric	2.5 ml
	Salt and pepper	
2 tbsp	Natural yogurt	2x15 ml
1 oz	Tamarind	25 g
1	Large onion	1
1 tbsp	Ground coriander	15 ml
4 tbsp	Oil	4x15 ml
12 oz	Ripe tomatoes	350 g
1 tbsp	Vinegar	15 ml
3	Cardamom pods	3
	Grated nutmeg	
1 tbsp	Chopped parsley	15 ml

Prick cod steaks and coat with flour. Leave for 10 minutes.

Peel and crush garlic and pound with turmeric and a little salt to a paste. Stir in yogurt. Wash fish steaks and spread with yogurt mixture. Marinate for 30 minutes.

Meanwhile, soak tamarind in ½ pint (300 ml) warm water. Squeeze till water becomes thick and brown, then strain.

Peel and finely chop onion. Pound with coriander, pepper and 1 tbsp (15 ml) oil to a paste. Blanch, peel and quarter tomatoes.

Put vinegar into a bowl with ½ pint (300 ml) water. Dip fish steaks into bowl to wash away yogurt. Pat dry with kitchen paper, then rub with onion paste.

Heat remaining oil in flameproof casserole and fry fish steaks for 3 minutes each side. Add tamarind water, tomatoes, cardamom pods, a pinch of nutmeg and a little salt. Cover and simmer gently for 15 minutes till fish is tender. Discard cardamom pods and sprinkle with parsley.

Fried fish with rougail

Overall timing 40 minutes plus overnight soaking

Freezing Not suitable

To serve 6

12 oz	Dried salt cod	350 g
1 lb	Ripe tomatoes	450 g
2	Fresh green chillies	2
3	Large onions	3
1 oz	Lard	25 g
¼ teasp	Ground ginger	1.25 ml
	Salt and pepper	
7 tbsp	Olive oil	7 x 15 ml
4 tbsp	Vinegar	4 x 15 ml

Soak the cod in cold water overnight.

Next day, make the rougail. Blanch, peel and chop the tomatoes. Deseed and slice the chillies. Peel and thinly slice one onion. Melt the lard in a saucepan, add the onion and fry till transparent. Add tomatoes with the chillies, ginger and salt. Bring to the boil. Simmer for 20 minutes till thick and pulpy.

Meanwhile, prepare the fish. Rinse fish under cold water and cut into cubes, discarding the skin and bones. Peel and chop remaining onions. Heat 6 tbsp (6x15 ml) oil in a frying pan and add onions and fish. Fry over a moderate heat for about 15 minutes, turning and mashing the fish, till crisp and brown. Stir in the vinegar and season to taste.

Arrange fish in a warmed serving dish. Stir remaining olive oil into rougail and adjust seasoning to taste. Pour over the fish and serve.

Beef and dhal curry

Overall timing 2¼ hours

Freezing Not suitable

To serve 4

4 oz	Egyptian lentils	125 g
¾ pint	Water	400 ml
2	Dried chillies	2
1½ lb	Chuck steak	700 g
2	Medium onions	2
1	Garlic clove	1
2 oz	Butter or ghee	50 g
2	Cardamom pods	2
2	Cloves	2
2 inch	Cinnamon stick	5 cm
1 tbsp	Curry powder	15 ml
1 tbsp	Tomato purée	15 ml
¼ pint	Tamarind water (see page 78)	150 ml
	Salt	

Put lentils into a pan with water and deseeded chillies. Bring to the boil and simmer for 10 minutes.

Meanwhile, cut meat into large cubes. Peel and finely chop onions; peel and crush garlic. Melt fat in flameproof casserole, add onions and garlic and fry for 3 minutes. Lightly crush cardamom pods and add to pan with other spices and curry powder. Fry gently, stirring, for 3 minutes.

Drain the lentils, reserving the liquid. Discard the chillies.

Stir tomato purée and meat into casserole and fry till coated with spice mixture. Add cooking liquor from lentils. Bring to the boil, cover and simmer gently for about 1½ hours till beef is tender.

Add lentils and tamarind water and simmer, uncovered, for a further 15 minutes till lentils become mushy and absorb the liquid. Discard cinnamon, cardamom and cloves. Add salt to taste, then serve with boiled rice.

Lentil meatballs

Overall timing 45 minutes

Freezing Suitable: reheat meatballs, covered, in 400°F (200°C) Gas 6 oven for 45 minutes

To serve 4–6

8 oz	Egyptian lentils	225 g
1	Small onion	1
2	Fresh green chillies	2
1 lb	Minced beef	450 g
1 teasp	Ground cumin	5 ml
	Salt and pepper	
8 oz	Long grain rice	225 g
4 tbsp	Oil	4x15 ml
1 tbsp	Chopped parsley	15 ml

Put 4 oz (125 g) of the lentils into a saucepan, cover with water and bring to the boil. Cover and simmer for 15 minutes.

Meanwhile, peel and chop the onion. Deseed and chop the chillies. Add onion and chillies to mince with the cumin and seasoning.

Drain the lentils and add to the mince mixture. Mix well. Using floured hands, shape the mixture into about 20 balls about 1½ inches (4 cm) in diameter.

Bring another saucepan of salted water to the boil, add the rice and remaining uncooked lentils and simmer for about 15 minutes till tender.

Meanwhile, heat the oil in a large frying pan. Add the meatballs and fry for about 10 minutes, turning frequently, till crisp and brown. Drain on kitchen paper.

Drain rice and lentils and place on a warmed serving plate. Arrange the meatballs on top, sprinkle with chopped parsley and serve.

Lamb and sweet potato curry

Overall timing 1½ hours

Freezing Suitable

To serve 4

2 lb	Lean lamb	900 g
1	Large onion	1
1	Garlic clove	1
2 tbsp	Oil	2x15 ml
1 oz	Butter or ghee	25 g
1 tbsp	Curry powder	15 ml
2	Thin slices of root ginger	2
1 oz	Plain flour	25 g
¼ pint	Natural yogurt	150 ml
¾ pint	Water	400 ml
12 oz	Sweet potatoes	350 g
	Salt	

Cut lamb into 1 inch (2.5 cm) pieces. Peel and finely chop the onion. Peel and crush garlic. Heat oil with butter or ghee in a flameproof casserole and fry onion with garlic till transparent. Add the curry powder and shredded ginger and fry, stirring, for 3 minutes.

Add the meat and fry till browned on all sides. Sprinkle in the flour and cook, stirring, for 3–4 minutes. Gradually add the yogurt and water and bring to the boil. Cover and simmer for 45 minutes, stirring occasionally.

Peel and dice the sweet potato. Add to the casserole and simmer for a further 15 minutes. Taste and adjust the seasoning. Serve from the casserole with plain boiled rice.

Pakistan lamb korma

Overall timing 1½ hours plus overnight marination

Freezing Not suitable

To serve 6

2 lb	Boned leg of lamb	900 g
2	Garlic cloves	2
½ pint	Natural yogurt	300 ml
	Salt and pepper	
2 inch	Cinnamon stick	5 cm
1	Bay leaf	1
4	Cloves	4
8	Small cardamom pods	8
2 teasp	Cumin seeds	2x5 ml
2	Fresh chillies	2
2 oz	Butter or ghee	50 g
½ teasp	Ground ginger	2.5 ml

Cut the lamb into 2 inch (5 cm) pieces. Put into a bowl. Peel and crush garlic and add to bowl with yogurt and plenty of seasoning. Mix till coated. Cover and marinate overnight in a cool place.

Next day, put the lamb and marinade in a flameproof casserole with the cinnamon stick, bay leaf and cloves and bring to the boil. Simmer for about 1 hour, stirring frequently, till the meat has absorbed all the yogurt and is tender.

Roughly crush the cardamom pods and cumin seeds. Deseed the chillies.

Melt the fat in a frying pan and add the meat, cardamom, cumin, chillies and ground ginger. Fry, stirring, over a low heat for about 10 minutes till the meat is brown and has a crusty coating. Adjust the seasoning and serve.

Curried lamb

Overall timing 1¾ hours

Freezing Suitable

To serve 4

2½ lb	Middle neck stewing lamb	1.1 kg
2	Onions	2
3 oz	Butter or ghee	75 g
2 tbsp	Plain flour	2x15 ml
1 tbsp	Curry powder	15 ml
1 pint	Stock	560 ml
2 oz	Desiccated coconut	50 g
	Salt and pepper	

Chop lamb into smallish pieces. Peel and finely slice the onions. Melt the fat in a flameproof casserole. Add the lamb and brown on all sides. Add the onions and fry till transparent. Sprinkle in the flour and curry powder and cook for about 3 minutes, stirring all the time.

Gradually stir in the stock. Bring to the boil, stirring. Add the coconut and seasoning. Cover and simmer for 1 hour till meat is tender. Adjust seasoning and serve with plain boiled rice.

Indian lamb steaks

Overall timing 30 minutes

Freezing Not suitable

To serve 4

1 lb	Aubergines	450 g
6 tbsp	Oil	6x15 ml
4x8 oz	Lamb steaks	4x225 g
	Salt and pepper	
2	Onions	2
8 oz	Cooking apples	225 g
1 oz	Butter or ghee	25 g
1 tbsp	Mild curry powder	15 ml
6 tbsp	Hot stock	6x15 ml
4 fl oz	Carton of single cream	113 ml
2 tbsp	Mango chutney	2x15 ml
	Pinch of sugar	

Slice the aubergines. Heat half the oil in a frying pan and fry aubergines very gently for 5 minutes on each side. Remove from pan, drain, then arrange round edge of warmed serving plate. Keep hot.

Cut each lamb steak in half and season. Add rest of oil to frying pan and when hot, fry lamb for 5 minutes on each side. Remove lamb and arrange on serving dish with aubergines. Keep hot.

Peel and finely chop onions. Peel, core and finely chop apples. Melt fat in a saucepan and cook onions and apples, stirring, for 4 minutes until light brown. Sprinkle in the curry powder and mix well. Place half of this mixture on the serving dish and stir stock, cream and chutney into the rest. Cook gently for a few minutes. Do not boil. Season with salt and sugar, then pour into sauceboat and serve separately.

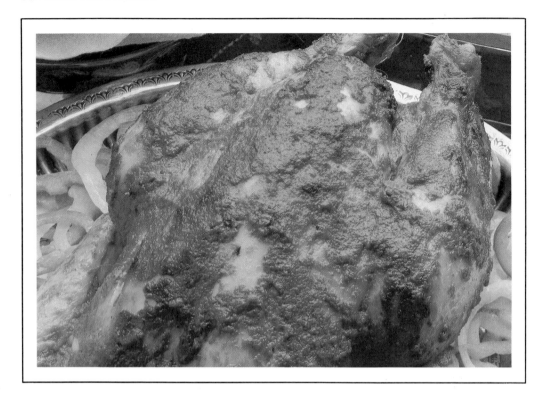

Tandoori chicken

Overall timing 2¼ hours plus overnight marination

Freezing Not suitable

To serve 4

2½ lb	Ovenready chicken	1.1 kg
1 teasp	Sea-salt	5 ml
8 tbsp	Lemon juice	8x15 ml
2	Garlic cloves	2
¼ teasp	Cayenne pepper	1.25 ml
¼ teasp	Chilli powder	1.25 ml
1 teasp	Ground coriander	5 ml
½ teasp	Ground cumin	2.5 ml
½ teasp	Curry powder	2.5 ml
¼ teasp	Ground turmeric	1.25 ml
2 tbsp	Natural yogurt	2x15 ml
2 tbsp	Tomato purée	2x15 ml
1 tbsp	Wine vinegar	15 ml
2 tbsp	Oil	2x15 ml
1 oz	Butter or ghee	25 g
2	Large onions	2
3	Green peppers	3

Make incisions all over chicken. Rub with salt and sprinkle with half lemon juice. Leave 30 minutes. Mix together peeled and crushed garlic, spices, yogurt, tomato purée, vinegar and 1 tbsp (15 ml) oil. Spread over chicken and leave in refrigerator overnight.

The next day, preheat the oven to 400°F (200°C) Gas 6. Place chicken on a rack in roasting tin and roast for 25 minutes till golden. Reduce temperature to 325°F (170°C) Gas 3. Baste chicken with marinade added to juices from roasting tin. Melt fat, pour over chicken and roast for 1 hour.

Peel onions and slice into rings. Deseed and slice peppers. Heat remaining oil in frying pan and fry onions and peppers till just tender.

Place chicken on warmed serving dish. Surround with onions and peppers and sprinkle with rest of lemon juice.

Chicken curry

Overall timing 1¼ hours

Freezing Suitable: add cream after reheating

To serve 4–6

2	Bananas	2
1	Apple	1
1	Garlic clove	1
2	Onions	2
2	Stalks of celery	2
3	Tomatoes	3
2 oz	Butter or ghee	50 g
3 lb	Chicken joints	1.4 kg
2 tbsp	Curry powder	2x15 ml
1 tbsp	Plain flour	15 ml
	Salt and pepper	
4 fl oz	Carton of single cream	113 ml
	Flaked almonds	

Peel and finely chop bananas, apple, garlic and onions. Trim and finely chop celery. Blanch, peel and chop tomatoes. Melt fat in a large frying pan, add onions, garlic and chicken joints and cook for a few minutes. Sprinkle with curry powder and flour and cook for 2 minutes, then season and stir in 4 fl oz (120 ml) water. Add tomatoes, celery, fruit and seasoning. Cover and cook for 45 minutes.

Remove chicken joints from pan and keep warm on a serving plate. Boil the sauce for 5 minutes, then reduce heat and stir in the cream. Heat through but do not boil. Strain sauce, if liked, and pour over chicken. Sprinkle with flaked almonds and serve with pilau rice. Serve separate dishes of grated coconut, lime pickle, mango chutney and banana slices.

Spiced chicken

Overall timing 1½ hours

Freezing Suitable: add cream after reheating

To serve 4–6

12 oz	Desiccated coconut	350 g
3 lb	Chicken joints	1.4 kg
2	Medium onions	2
4 tbsp	Oil	4x15 ml
2 teasp	Curry powder	2x5 ml
1 teasp	Ground mace	5 ml
1 pint	Chicken stock	560 ml
	Bouquet garni	
3 tbsp	Single cream	3x15 ml
	Salt and pepper	

Put coconut in saucepan with ¼ pint (150 ml) water. Bring to the boil, then cool. Squeeze coconut for about 1 minute so that water turns white. Strain liquid and reserve. Repeat process with another ¼ pint (150 ml) water three times to make 1 pint (560 ml) coconut milk.

Cut chicken into small pieces. Peel and finely chop onions. Heat oil in saucepan, add onions and cook till transparent. Add curry powder and mace and cook, stirring, for 2 minutes. Add chicken pieces and stir-fry over high heat for 10–15 minutes till golden on all sides. Reduce heat and stir in stock, coconut milk and bouquet garni. Cover and cook for 45 minutes, stirring occasionally.

Remove chicken pieces with a draining spoon, place on a warmed serving dish and keep hot. Discard bouquet garni. Reduce sauce by half by boiling. Sieve and return to pan. Stir in cream. Stir over gentle heat till sauce is smooth and heated through. Taste and adjust seasoning. Either pour sauce over chicken or serve separately in a sauce boat.

Chicken biriani

Overall timing 1¾ hours

Freezing Not suitable

To serve 6

3 lb	Ovenready chicken	1.4 kg
1	Garlic clove	1
1 inch	Piece of root ginger	2.5 cm
1	Green pepper	1
2	Fresh green chillies	2
2 inch	Cinnamon stick	5 cm
	Salt and pepper	
3 oz	Butter or ghee	75 g
8 oz	Long grain rice	225 g
4	Cardamom pods	4
4	Cloves	4
1 tbsp	Ground turmeric	15 ml
1 tbsp	Ground coriander	15 ml
½ teasp	Cayenne pepper	2.5 ml
1 tbsp	Ground cumin	15 ml
1 teasp	Indian poppy seeds	5 ml
2	Onions	2

Cut chicken into joints and put into a saucepan with 1¼ pints (700 ml) cold water. Peel garlic; finely chop ginger. Deseed and thinly slice pepper and chillies. Add all to pan with cinnamon and seasoning. Cover and simmer for about 45 minutes till chicken is tender. Remove chicken and cool. Strain stock.

Melt 1 oz (25 g) fat in a saucepan. Stir in rice, lightly crushed cardamom pods and cloves and fry, stirring, for 3 minutes. Mix remaining spices together and add half to rice with 1 pint (560 ml) reserved stock. Simmer for 15 minutes till rice is tender.

Meanwhile, cut chicken into neat pieces, discarding skin and bones. Peel onions and cut into wedges. Melt remaining fat in a frying pan and fry onions for 5 minutes. Add remaining spice mixture and chicken and cook for 5 minutes. Stir into rice and cook for 5 minutes.

Madras vegetable curry

Overall timing 40 minutes

Freezing Not suitable

To serve 4–6

2	Large onions	2
2	Garlic cloves	2
3 oz	Butter or ghee	75 g
1 tbsp	Hot curry powder	15 ml
1 teasp	Ground turmeric	5 ml
1 lb	Waxy potatoes	450 g
1 lb	Okra	450 g
4	Large ripe tomatoes	4
2 oz	Creamed coconut	50 g
1 pint	Water	560 ml
	Salt and pepper	

Peel and finely chop the onions. Peel and crush the garlic. Melt the fat in a large saucepan, add the onion and garlic and fry till transparent. Sprinkle the curry powder and turmeric over and cook gently for 2 minutes.

Peel and quarter the potatoes. Trim the okra. Add to the pan and fry gently, stirring, for 5 minutes. Quarter the tomatoes and add to the pan with the creamed coconut, water and salt. Bring to the boil and simmer gently for about 15 minutes till the potatoes are tender.

Taste and adjust seasoning. Arrange in a warmed serving dish and serve with pilau rice.

Pilau rice

Overall timing 45 minutes plus soaking

Freezing Not suitable

To serve 4-6

1 lb	Patna rice	450 g
1	Large onion	1
1	Garlic clove	1
6	Whole allspice	6
8	Cardamom pods	8
4 oz	Butter or ghee	125 g
2 inch	Cinnamon stick	5 cm
8	Cloves	8
1 teasp	Ground turmeric	5 ml
	Salt	
2 oz	Flaked almonds	50 g
4 oz	Sultanas	125 g

Soak rice in cold water for 1 hour, then drain thoroughly.

Peel and finely chop the onion. Peel and crush garlic. Lightly crush allspice and cardamom pods. Melt 3 oz (75 g) of the fat in a saucepan. Add onion, garlic and spices and fry till onion is transparent but not browned.

Add rice and cook over a low heat, stirring, for 3–4 minutes. Add salt to taste and enough boiling water to come 1 inch (2.5 cm) above the rice. Cover pan tightly and simmer over a very low heat for about 20 minutes till water is absorbed and rice is tender.

Melt remaining fat in frying pan and fry almonds and sultanas for 3–5 minutes. Mix lightly into rice and serve immediately.

Pakistan turnip purée

Overall timing 35 minutes

Freezing Not suitable

To serve 4–6

1½ lb	Turnips	700 g
	Salt and pepper	
1	Medium onion	1
1 oz	Butter or ghee	25 g
1 teasp	Ground cumin	5 ml
½ teasp	Ground fenugreek	2.5 ml
1 tbsp	Chopped onion	15 ml
1 teasp	Chopped parsley	5 ml

Peel the turnips and cut into 1 inch (2.5 cm) chunks. Put into a saucepan of lightly salted cold water and bring to the boil. Cover and simmer for about 15 minutes till tender. Drain well.

Peel and finely chop the onion. Melt the fat in the saucepan and fry the onion gently till transparent. Add the cumin, fenugreek and ¼ teasp (1.25 ml) pepper and cook over a low heat for 2 minutes, stirring.

Return the turnips to the pan. Cover and cook for 5 minutes, shaking the pan occasionally. Mash the turnips to a smooth purée. Adjust the seasoning and pile in a warmed serving dish. Garnish with chopped raw onion and parsley and serve.

Dhal with spinach

Overall timing 45 minutes

Freezing Suitable: reheat, adding a knob of butter

To serve 4–6

8 oz	Egyptian lentils	225 g
1 pint	Water	560 ml
2	Fresh chillies	2
1	Onion	1
1	Garlic clove	1
2 oz	Butter or ghee	50 g
½ teasp	Ground cumin	2.5 ml
1 teasp	Ground turmeric	5 ml
	Salt	
1 lb	Spinach	450 g

Put the lentils into a large saucepan with the water and bring to the boil. Reduce heat and simmer for 25 minutes.

Meanwhile, deseed and finely chop the chillies. Peel and finely chop the onion. Peel and crush garlic. Melt fat in a small saucepan and fry the onion with the garlic, spices and salt for 5 minutes.

Add spinach and chillies to lentils and cook for 5 minutes. Stir spiced onion mixture into lentils, cover and cook for a further 5–10 minutes. Taste and adjust seasoning before serving.

Chickpea fritters

Overall timing 30 minutes

Freezing Not suitable

To serve 4

1 teasp	Dried yeast	5 ml
¼ pint	Lukewarm milk	150 ml
8 oz	Chickpea flour	225 g
½ teasp	Salt	2.5 ml
¼ teasp	Dried marjoram	1.25 ml
	Oil for deep frying	
	Pepper	

Blend together the yeast and warm milk and leave to stand for 10 minutes or till mixture begins to froth.

Put the flour in a bowl and make a well in the centre. Pour yeast mixture into the bowl, add salt and marjoram and mix to a soft batter, adding a little more warm water if necessary.

Heat the oil in a deep-fryer to 340°F (170°C). Drop the batter a few spoonfuls at a time into the hot fat. Cook until puffy and golden brown, turning fritters over once or twice. Remove from pan and drain on kitchen paper. Season with pepper and serve hot.

Bhugias

Overall timing 25 minutes

Freezing Not suitable

Makes 12

4 oz	Plain flour	125 g
1 teasp	Salt	5 ml
¼ teasp	Chilli powder	1.25 ml
2 teasp	Ground turmeric	2x5 ml
2	Eggs	2
4 tbsp	Milk	4x15 ml
1 lb	Onions	450 g
	Oil for frying	

Sift the flour, salt, chilli powder and turmeric into a large bowl. Make a well in the centre. Add the eggs and stir with a wooden spoon, gradually drawing the flour into the liquid. Add the milk and mix to a thick batter.

Peel and thinly slice the onions. Stir into the batter.

Heat the oil in a deep-fryer to 340°F (170°C). Carefully lower rounded spoonfuls of the batter mixture into the hot oil and fry for about 3 minutes each side till puffed and deep golden. Drain on kitchen paper and serve hot with curries or stews.

Spicy braised cauliflower

Overall timing 25 minutes

Freezing Not suitable

To serve 4

1	Large cauliflower	1
1	Onion	1
1 inch	Piece of root ginger	2.5 cm
2 oz	Butter or ghee	50 g
2 teasp	Mustard seeds	2x5 ml
1 tbsp	Ground turmeric	15 ml
½ pint	Chicken stock	300 ml
	Salt and pepper	

Trim cauliflower and cut into large florets. Peel and finely chop the onion. Finely chop the ginger.

Melt the fat in a saucepan, add onion and fry till transparent. Increase the heat, add the mustard seeds and shake the pan over a low heat until they start to pop. Stir in ginger and turmeric and cook for 30 seconds.

Add the cauliflower and stir till coated with the spices, then pour in the stock. Season and bring to the boil. Cover and simmer for about 10 minutes till florets are just tender.

Taste and adjust seasoning and serve immediately with plain boiled rice.

Curried vegetables

Overall timing 1½ hours

Freezing Not suitable

To serve 4

1	Large onion	1
1	Garlic clove	1
3 tbsp	Oil	3x15 ml
2 teasp	Curry powder	2x5 ml
1 teasp	Ground coriander	5 ml
10	Small ripe tomatoes *or*	10
8 oz	Can of tomatoes	227 g
8 oz	Carrots	225 g
4 oz	Beans	125 g
1	Yellow pepper	1
2 oz	Button onions	50 g
4 oz	Frozen peas	125 g
	Salt	

Peel and finely chop large onion; peel and crush garlic. Heat oil in frying pan and add onion and garlic. Stir in curry powder and coriander and cook for about 10 minutes till onions are soft, adding a little water if they begin to stick.

Blanch, peel and finely chop fresh tomatoes, or drain and mash canned tomatoes, reserving juice. Add tomato pulp to pan and cook for 15 minutes over a high heat.

Peel carrots and cut into strips. Add with beans to pan. Reduce heat and cook for a further 15 minutes.

Deseed and chop pepper and add to pan with ½ pint (300 ml) stock (or juice from can of tomatoes), peeled button onions and peas and cook for 15 minutes more over a moderate heat. Season with salt.

Index